Education
in
the Emerging India

Education
in
the Emerging India

R.P. Pathak

ATLANTIC

PUBLISHERS & DISTRIBUTORS (P) LTD

ATLANTIC
PUBLISHERS & DISTRIBUTORS (P) LTD

7/22, Ansari Road, Darya Ganj, New Delhi
Tel.: +91-11-4077 5252, 2327 3880
E-mail: orders@atlanticbooks.com
Web: www.atlanticbooks.com

This edition published in 2024 by Atlantic Publishers & Distributors (P) Ltd.

Reprint 2021

Printed & bound in India by Atlantic Print Services

Preface

Education is a dynamic process. It changes with the changing of socio-politico-economic conditions and fast expanding knowledge over the years. The fundamental purpose of education is to secure for everyone the conditions under which individuality is most completely developed. The content of education and consequently, the development of personality are both conditioned by the Philosophy and Sociology of education. The impact of socio-economic and political conditions on the life of the individuals and communities has been striking.

The need for reconstructing education was never so urgent and acute as it is today. Education must enshrine all what is good and noble, what is socially significant, and lead to the emancipation and proper equipment of the individual to promote the well-being of society of which he/she is an integral part. This book is a humble attempt in this direction and also provides excellent national perspectives on several emerging issues unravelling relationships between education and development in Indian society.

Structured into six chapters, the present book studies in depth the concept and nature of education, its approaches and dimensions, history and development. Besides these, it studies the trends, processes, ideals and philosophy of education against the backdrop of Indian society. Above all, the book analytically presents the elements, mission and aspirations of Indian society. The bibliography included in the book will prove a useful study-aid to readers to pursue the study further. Overall, the book is highly useful to the students and researchers of Education.

I am thankful to numerous authors whom I have quoted at different places in the book. I acknowledge the co-operation extended to me by several friends and colleagues in the preparation of this book. I am especially indebted to my teacher for his kind help and guidance. I take this opportunity to put on record my deep sense of gratitude to my Vice Chancellor, Prof. Vachaspati Upadhyay, who always inspired me. I must express my thanks to my wife without whose encouragement, devotion and sacrifice the publication of this book would not have been possible. I also thank to my M.Ed. and Ph.D. students. They taught me more than they may realise. I am grateful to Dr. K.R. Gupta, Chairman, Atlantic Publishers and Distributors (P) Ltd., New Delhi, for his co-operation in the publication of the book.

R.P. Pathak

Contents

Concept and Nature of Education

1

Education has always played an important role in shaping the destinies of societies through development of the whole individual and linking education to the task of social upliftment and national development within a highly competitive global scenario. The Indian nation is striving to build a society of humane, committed, participative and productive citizens who can shoulder the task of building an enlightened, strong and prosperous country. Modern India is a multicultural and multilingual society with an undercurrent of essential unity. Some of the important national goals as enshrined in the Constitution are: secularism, democracy, equality, liberty, fraternity, justice, national integration and patriotism. Education today has the enormous task of the upliftment of the underprivileged and their empowerment.

It is widely accepted that education, adequate in quality and scale, is the most powerful instrument for achieving goals of economic development, technological progress and also for establishing social cohesion. Education tends to create a social order based on values of freedom, social justice and equal opportunity. Simultaneously, it also fosters a deeper and harmonious form of human development which leads to reduction in poverty, ignorance, oppression and war. Education brings about modification of behaviour in an individual through his continuous and intensive interaction with the environment.

Education, by its very nature, influences and gets influenced by the total developmental process. However, the content and process of education need to be continuously renewed in order to keep them in tune with the changing needs, aspirations and demands of the society. Thus, education and society are interdependent and each reinforces the other. According to John Dewey, 'Education is not a preparation for life but life itself'. In this sense education and life are inseparable. Education begins with wonder: a thrill of the mysterious. Native human urge of curiosity drives the mind to unravel the mystery of the unknown.

MEANING AND NATURE OF EDUCATION

Definition of Education

From Socrates and Plato to Dewey and Gandhi the word education has been defined differently by different people. One set of definition lays stress on the inner potentialities of an individual. These definitions view education as the process of unfolding or developing what is innate in the child. Some definitions supporting this viewpoint are as follows:

- **Mahatma Gandhi.** By education, I mean an all round drawing out of the best in the child and man—body, mind and spirit.
- **Pestalozzi.** Education is the natural, harmonious and progressive development of man's innate powers.
- **Swami Vivekanand.** Education is the manifestation of divine perfection already existing in man.
- **Froebel.** Education is unfoldment of what is already unfolded in the germ. It is the process through which the child makes internal as external.
- **Sri Aurobindo.** Education is helping the growing soul to draw out what is in itself.

Another set of definition considers education as a lifelong process comprising all the influences, viz. physical, social and cultural which act upon the individual. From this viewpoint, education signifies all the life experiences which lead to the modification of behaviour.

In this context the definition of education given by John Dewey is most relevant. It defines education as: The development of all those capacities in the individual which will enable him to control his environment and fulfil his possibilities.

In addition to the above, we may like to consider some more definitions which throw light on other aspects of education:

- **Rousseau.** Education is a positive approach which is given to the child and which is intended to shape his mind. It is intended to teach him the duties of adults.
- ***Rigveda.*** Education is something which makes a man self-reliant and selfless.
- ***Upanishads.*** Education is something which liberates man from all bondage.
- **Tagore.** Education is that which makes one's life in harmony with all existence and thus enables the mind to find the ultimate truth which gives us the wealth of inner light and significance to life.
- **Education Commission (1964-66).** Education ought to be related to the life, needs and aspirations of the people and thereby made a powerful instrument of social, economic and cultural transformation.
- **NPE (1986).** Education is fundamental to our all round development, material and spiritual. It is a unique investment in the present and the future.
- **Delor's Commission (1996).** Education is one of the principal means available to foster a deeper and more harmonious form of human development and thereby reduce poverty, exclusion, ignorance, oppression and war.

Meaning of Education

The meaning of education can be understood in a narrow sense or in a broader or comprehensive perspective.

Indian Concept of Education

सा विद्या या विमुक्तये, i.e. education which emancipates. Education fails if it does not help the individual to cultivate the art of life. Tagore in *Gitanjali* dreamt of the heaven of freedom in which "the mind is without fear and the head is held high". True liberty is attained by self-discipline directed to the conquest by the mind's six enemies namely desire, anger, greed, attachment, intemperance and jealousy. Good education enables a person to understand other men, their thinking and actions. According to

Bhagwat Gita, what distinguishes a cultured mind is that it is a *Samadarshi*, i.e. see all as equal.

Philosophy of Education

Education primarily depends upon the aspects of man's nature that are relevant to the formulation of valid educational ideals. These ideals of education differ from community to community and from country to country, depending upon the goals which they are expected to achieve. The objectives of education differ from one stage of an individual's growth to another stage.

As discussed earlier education aims at development of the whole individual or total personality of the child so that it can contribute to the enrichment of human life and society. As Dewey has stated "Education is the development of those capacities in the individual which will enable him to control his environment and fulfil his possibilities".

This is where Philosophical foundations of education become relevant. Philosophy endeavours to understand all that comes within the scope of human experience. Philosophy is a search for a comprehensive view of nature. It attempts at explaining the nature of the universe and man and their mutual relationship.

Metaphysics: Philosophy is an intellectual exercise based on reason. It studies the nature of reality.

Epistemology: The nature of knowledge.

Axiology: The nature of values. The system of education in any country is influenced by the philosophy of its own nation.

Dr. Radhakrishnan has defined philosophy as critical exposition of reality. It is not merely a bookish knowledge but the result of logical thinking and contemplation. An understanding of the philosophical base helps the educationist to:

- decide the objectives,
- design learning outcomes,
- select appropriate methods of teaching,
- prepare the curriculum and take other important decisions in education.

Therefore, education is described as the dynamic side of philosophy. Philosophy provides the ideas and ideals which are transformed into action by education. Any outcome of education attains complete clarity only with the help of philosophy.

The educational philosophers—both Western and Indian have been keen observers and analysers of the human nature. They have articulated these observations in a highly instructive manner. These careful and systematic approach to ideas fostered by the philosophers have greatly aided education to gain inspiration and develop insights into the complex educational problems. Philosophy, reflects upon questions like—who are we? What are we doing? Why are we doing? How are we to justify our doings? We might say philosophy helps an educator to gain a wider and deeper perspective about the world around.

Philosophy as an Investigator

Educational philosophy analyses the problems of education from the point of view of philosophy, e.g. philosophical considerations play an important role in curriculum construction. Objectives of education and teaching methods are natural results of philosophical principles. In other words, philosophy acts as an investigator of educational experiments. Different philosophies of idealism, realism, naturalism, pragmatism look to the total teaching and learning system from their own points of view.

Idealism

Idealism gives special stress on spiritual development and self realization. Education leads to character formation and inculcation of eternal ideals and values. The ultimate ends which man must seek are virtue and wisdom or truth, goodness and beauty. According to Idealism the main aim of education is cultivation of moral values. Education must help the individual to develop his physical, intellectual, social, moral and spiritual potentialities completely. Man must conserve his cultural heritage and also enrich it by adding something of his own.

Realism

Realism is primarily concerned with the world as it is here and now. To a realist, senses are the doors of knowledge.

Knowledge of society, science and nature including vocational education are stressed. Realism gives predominance to first hand experience rather than bookish knowledge. All knowledge is derived from experience. Man is born without any inherent ideas. Locke, the founder of comprehensive realism placed greatest reliance upon immediate experience and sense perception. He emphasised the disciplinary approach to education. According to him, three aspects of education are: physical, moral and intellectual. Corresponding aims of education are therefore, vigour of body virtue and knowledge.

Naturalism

Naturalism gives importance to the child and child centred education. It stresses the importance of empirical knowledge. It focuses its attention to direct experience with nature without the interference of the teacher or society. Naturalists believe that everything that comes from nature is pure, but the civilised society pollutes it. According to them, the first thing is to understand the nature of the child and then accordingly provide him/her the facilities and opportunities to develop. Romantic naturalists believe in complete development of the child through direct contact with nature. Evolutionary naturalists say that education should enable the child to adjust to the changing conditions of society while experimental naturalists stress on the study of science and scientific method. Naturalists advocate play way method in earlier stages. Rigidity of time table is not acceptable to them. Teacher's role becomes that of a facilitator and observer. The child learns through his free choice, participation in activities and by his/her direct experience with nature.

Pragmatism

Pragmatism stressed the utilitarian aspect of the knowledge and experiences. The potentialities of the child are to be developed through education with a view to making him a useful citizen of the society. To a pragmatist truth is that which works, it is not absolute. Child creates values out of his own experience. The basic purpose of school is to train the pupils in co-operative living. According to Dewey, a great exponent of Pragmatism education helps:

- the process of reconstruction of experience, and
- gives it a socialised value through increased individual efficiency.

The school should provide enough freedom to the child and also facilitate his learning from his own experience. Activities undertaken will be instrumental to individual and social needs. The project method is the contribution of pragmatism to education. Thus, in spirit, Pragmatism is naturalistic in method, it is scientific and practical and in purpose, it is social and human.

EDUCATIONAL THOUGHTS OF INDIAN THINKERS TO EDUCATION

Educational thought of Mahatma Gandhi

Gandhiji's contribution to education is best known through his scheme called *NAI-TALIM* or Basic Education. He argued that education must begin not with the children but with the parent and the community. He gave the concept of learning by doing. Basic education aimed at a social order free from exploitation and violence. The fundamental objective was the development of child's total personality including productive efficiency. Basic Education postulates that the curricular content should be intelligently related to three main centres of correlation, viz. craft work, the natural environment and the social environment.

Educational thought of Rabindra Nath Tagore

Tagore's ideas regarding the individual and his development are similar to that of Rousseau. According to him, each person is different from the other and everyone is unique. To him, the object of education is the freedom of mind. Tagore emphasised the activity method. The natural environment provided him the teaching-learning material. Learning by the child should essentially be explorative, active and full of joy.

Educational thought of Sri Aurobindo

Sri Aurobindo said, "the first principle of true teaching is that nothing can be taught. The teacher is not an instructor or task master, he is a helper and a guide. His business is to suggest and not to impose". The teacher enables the child to acquire knowledge for himself. Everyone has in him something divine, something his own, a chance of perfection. The task of education is to find it, develop it and use it. Like Gandhiji Sri Aurobindo also stated that the main aim of education should be to help the growing soul to draw out that in itself which is best and make it perfect for a noble cause. According to Sri Aurobindo, a free and natural growth is in the condition of genuine development.

PHILOSOPHY INFLUENCES EDUCATION

Aims of Education

Philosophy has an effective bearing on the aims of education. It determines and resolves questions like:

- whether aim of education should be intellectual development or moral perfection,
- whether education should be vocational or liberal,
- whether education should be for the development and happiness of the individual or for the good of the society?

Curriculum

Curriculum is the means for realising the aims of education. The aims of education, in turn are derived from the general aim of life which is determined by philosophy. The Nation's philosophy at a given time determines the curriculum to meet the emerging needs of the society.

Methods of Teaching

The nature of the method of teaching is determined by the aim and as seen earlier aims of education are determined by philosophy. Thus, methods of teaching also get determined by the prevailing philosophy. It is through the method that a teacher establishes contact with the child for transacting the given subject matter. Pragmatism which advocates learning by doing has given Project method. Methods of enquiry and discovery are important from the point of view of Idealism. Realism is focussed on Empirical method. Thus, different philosophies of education advocated different methods of teaching.

Discipline

The nature of discipline too is determined by the philosophy, e.g. Naturalism stands for freedom of the child, Idealism relies much on the personality of the teacher for maintenance of discipline. Pragmatism does not believe in imposing external discipline. The Idealistic viewpoint that strict discipline is necessary to make the child a good citizen is refuted by the pragmatists. They also favour freedom.

Teacher

The vital belief or outlook towards life of a teacher affects the problems of education, the learner, the aims of education and their realization. It also influences the nature of discipline to be maintained, social organization of the school, general ethos and methods he/she employs. We might have seen by now that education may be termed as an applied branch of the philosophy. If philosophy and education are considered as two sides of the same coin, then philosophy will identify with the contemplative side while education with the active side.

Aims of Education

Education is a purposeful activity. It has certain aims which serve as the frame of reference. The aims of education may be broadly categorised as:

- Individualistic aims
- Social aims.

Individualistic Aims of Education

Individualistic aims relate to the development of the individual his intellect, power of judgement, self reliance, health and hygiene and other similar attributes necessary for a balanced and harmonious development of the personality. As Kant put it—"Education is the development in the individual of all the perfection of which he is capable".

Social Aims of Education

An individual cannot be conceived in isolation from society. Man being a social person, the main aim of education should be to develop this person as a useful, productive and effective citizen. It is in this context that Gandhiji said, "Willing submission to social control and restraint for the sake of the well being of the whole society enriches both the individual and the society of which the former is a member. The vocational efficiency, training for citizenship, training for leisure and prepartion of the individual for adult life are all social in nature. The individual is to develop himself for the needs and demands of the society".

As a matter of fact individual and social aims are complementary to each other. The interest of the State or society can be promoted only by the development of the individual. The real aim of education therefore, may be stated as the highest development of an individual as a member of the society. The individual and the society should work for a common objective.

Classification of Aims

Aims of education may be classified as follows:

Acquiring Knowledge

Acquiring knowledge is an important aim of education. It lays more stress on cognitive or intellective development. Knowledge is to be acquired for applying it to new situations for social and human upliftment. Knowledge helps the individual to adjust to and also master the environment. It is a potential power. Knowledge acts as an agent of promoting human welfare.

Character Formation

Another important aim of education is the building of a sound moral character by modifying the child's behaviour. Swami Vivekanand said, "the end of all education, all training should be man making". Education therefore, should cultivate the human values and ethical conduct. The personality and behaviour of teacher towards students play a key role in influencing the character formation. The teacher must set an example in this respect. Entire school environment must be made congenial and conducive to moral development. Parents and the society too play crucial role in character formation. True education shall have to take care of physical, social, intellectual and moral development of the individual.

Vocational Aim

Education must prepare a person to be self-reliant as far as the satisfaction of basic needs of food, shelter and clothing are concerned. In the present day world, education for livelihood has surfaced as the major aim of education. Much emphasis is being given to vocational, technical and professional education. The basic assumption in this context is that knowledge gained must be functional and applicable to the problems faced by the individual and the society. However, liberal education emphasising intellectual, moral and social development and vocational education aiming at economic and industrial progress are complementary to each other.

Overall Development Aim

Over emphasis on any one of the aims described in this section has the tendency to lead to lopsided development of personality. The aim of education should be the total and harmonious development of child's personality in all its dimensions namely: personal, social, emotional, spiritual, physical and aesthetic. According to Pestalozzi, "the sole aim of education is the harmonious development of the faculties and dispositions".

Leisure Aim

Modern labour saving devices, in addition to saving one from drudgery, create plenty of leisure. It is important, therefore, to know the various ways and means to utilize this leisure in a productive manner. Education should lead the child to utilization of latent talents, participate in creative activities and work for common good.

Contemporary Aims of Education

The Education Commission (1964-66) recommended the following aims of education to link education to the process of national development:

- Increasing productivity.
- Social and national integration.
- Modernization.
- Cultivation of social, moral and spiritual values.

The National Policy on Education (NPE) 1986, laid down the following aims keeping in view the contemporary realities and needs of the society:

- Evolving a national system of education and a common educational structure of 10+2+3 for the entire nation.
- Need for a common National Curriculum Framework with inbuilt flexibility to take care of regional needs and local diversities.
- Ten core components to be studied by all students are:
    - (i) the history of India's freedom movement,
    - (ii) the constitutional obligations,
    - (iii) nuturing of a national identity,
    - (iv) small family norm,
    - (v) gender equality,
    - (vi) common cultural heritage,
    - (vii) egalitarianism, democracy and socialism,
    - (viii) removal of social barriers,
    - (ix) conservation and protection of environment,
    - (x) scientific temper.
- Promoting world view of peace and understanding.
- Equality of educational opportunities.
- Development of diverse cultural and social systems.
- Facilitating inter-regional mobility.
- Strengthening areas of research and development.
- Lifelong education.

NPE 1986, regarded education as a unique investment which also has an acculturating role in society. It refines sensitivities and perceptions that contribute to national cohesiveness, a scientific temper and independence of mind and spirit. This is desirable for achieving the goal of socialism, secularism and democracy enshrined in the Indian Constitution.

Approaches and Dimensions of Education

2

In the emerging era of Information Technology revolution, the knowledge base is doubling every three months. A moment in human history has come for a new approach to education to enable the future generations to confront and overcome the tensions that they will face in the new millennium. These tensions are between the global and the local, the universal and the individual, the traditional and the modern. The expansion of knowledge and the human beings' capacity for assimilation and also the material growth have drawn attention of the society towards spiritual development.

New Approach to Education

The National Policy on Education states that 'there are moments in history when new direction has to be given to an age old process. That moment is today'. It further states that 'higher education provides people with an opportunity to reflect on the critical social, economic, cultural, moral and spiritual issues facing humanity. It contributes to the national development'. It also adds that, 'higher education has to become dynamic as never before'.

The 'explosion of knowledge' and 'technological revolution' of the modern time has amazingly affected all people across the globe and has left their dramatic influences on every field of human activity, be it our dress design, kitchen-wares, building patterns, mode of conveyance, communication system, life-style, food habits, recipes of the restaurant food, health care approach, professional choices, value system or thinking process. The change is taking place every where and that too with an ever increasing pace. In every field of life and work multiple options and alternatives are available.

Education in our country has been rather slow in accommodating the changes and adjusting the system accordingly. The images of a traditional 'guru' (master), 'disciple' and 'disciplinary process' is still occupying our attention, with little exception here and there. What is most required now, is changing the very mind-set of the people. Education being the most potent force in shaping the humanity, we must make it the most vibrant and dynamic force to respond to the changing requirements of time. Before studying the characteristics of education in the emerging society, let us first have an overview of the changes that have taken place in our conception of education over the years. Table 2.1 gives the changing concept of education as a result of the social changes.

Table 2.1: Types of Society

Types of Society	Salient Features/ Life	Needs	Nature of Learning/ Education	Pace of Learning/ Education
1	2	3	4	5
Primitive/ Hunting-Gathering	Erratic Nomadic Instinctive Fearful Trying	Primary, Physical, Food, Clothing, Shelter, Security Concrete Definite	Instantious, Accidental, Irregular, Disorganized, Personal	Very slow, long process.
Agricultural	Settled Inquisitive Patterned Natural Symbiotic Independent Easier Feudal-system	Physical Social Little Technical/ Calculative Limited	Observation-based Experimental Cumulative Experimental Social-organized, Co-operative	Slow
Industrial	Mechanical Competitive Urbanized Scientific Specialized Pragmatic Mass-based Imperialistic	Technical Organizational Exclusive Personal Psycho-social Ever-widening International	Experimental Imitative Informative Competitive Vocationalized Professionalized Inter-personal Group based	Fast

Contd...

Contd...

1	2	3	4	5
Post-Industrial (Emerging)	Tertial-sector Knowledge-based Individualistic Interactive	Global/Local/ Personal	Highly-informative Speculative Reflective Individualized Flexible Liberal	Very fast

Table 2.1 is quite indicative of how the nature of learning/ education changed with the evolution of society along with its changing needs and priorities. Education being a very complex term, it is rather difficult to arrive at a single uniform definition. When people change, their viewpoints also change and with their changing viewpoints education carries new meanings. That is why thinkers in the East and West try to define education differently. Before discussing the changing concepts of education, let us make an attempt now to understand the essential components of education.

Changing Components of Education

We may like to make a list of some of the components of education, as given below:

- Teacher
- Students
- Textbooks
- Schools/Colleges/ Universities
- Classrooms
- Teaching
- Reading
- Writing
- Listening
- Memorising
- Understanding
- Examination
- Achievement
- Success
- Failure
- Discipline
- Learning
- Forgetting, etc.

If we concentrate a little more and try to view education from different standpoints and at a deeper level we will surely be able to add many more components to the above list. We attempt to identify the components and understand the concept of education in the right direction. Education encompasses all these and many more aspects which sometimes are even beyond the reach of our minds too. But there is nothing wrong in trying to develop our own way of thinking and understanding education.

To facilitate the process, let us shortlist those components of education which we consider very vital and essential as under:

- Some Goals, Objectives and Aims
- Teachers
- Students
- Schools
- Curriculum
- Teaching/Curriculum Transaction
- Evaluation/Examination.

Taking all these components individually, if we make a quick comparative analysis between the past, present, and future, hopefully it will be insightful for all of us to have a feel of change everywhere, sometimes subtle and sometimes concrete. Let us study Table 2.2 to understand:

Table 2.2: Components of Education

Components of Education	Past	Present	Future
1	2	3	4
Goals/Aims/ Objectives	God-realization, Self-realization, Liberation. Definite-fixed	Gainful employment	Self-develop Need-fulfillment
Teachers	Next to God, Authoritarion, Full of wisdom, Men of character, Rigid	One among others, Flexible, Liberate, Still senior by age	Younger ones may be teachers. Any one who has information
Students	Disciplined, Obedient, Loyal, Age-specific	Liberal, Less formal rules	Little formal rules, Any one can be a student
Schools	Gurukulas, Specialized, Exist separately	School, College, University	Homes, Cyber Cafes, Any where
Teaching/ Learning Material	Initially None, Handwritten or Various Material printed	Desk-top printing	E-book, Virtual Book

Contd...

Contd...

1	2	3	4
Teaching/ Learning	Residential, Informal Life-oriented, Teacher centered	Student-centered, Non-Formal, Informal	Governed by the Learner
Evaluation/ Examination	Informal/Formal Terminal, Annual	Continuous evaluation. Peer group, Open-book External	Self-evaluation Governed by Learner

If we look at the present scenario of education, we will notice a sea of change everywhere. There has been a paradigm shift from the past to present. The goal of education has shifted from God-realization, liberation to gainful employment. Teachers are no more incarnations/parallels of God and men of sterling characters and that rigid type. Students are no longer that meek and obedient to their teachers. They are more likely to listen to the dictrates of their own wishes than that of the teachers. They are more keen to earn than learn. Schools are no more temples of learning as they earlier used to be. Though curriculum has remained relatively rigid over the years, yet a variety of courses have been added and the future curriculum is going to be totally different and diversified. It is more and more need-based, relevant and flexible. The titles of curriculum framework by NCERT and NCTE are significant and praiseworthy steps in this direction.

Teaching is going to be completely different from the past. With the advent of science and technology, i.e. TV, Computers, ET, Internet, Websites, CWC, distance education, on-line education, etc., education is at the threshold of a revolution. Learning shall not be a one-time job. It is being accepted as a life-long process.

There is no deadline for learning. Education for all, Total literacy campaign, Sarva Siksha Abhiyan, under the aegis of Adult and Non-formal education, are some indicators of the same phenomenon. Evaluation/Examination has shifted from being terminal or annual to continuous, comprehensive, self and peer evaluation rather than by an external agency like teacher or board of examination. Like learning, it will also be personal and dictated by the examinee.

Changes Associated and Likely

Education is undoubtedly more than just the sum total of its components. It is something holistic and the whole has always been greater than its parts. But that does not bring much difference in our understanding of education. Changes in the constituent parts or essential components of education is positively a change in education itself.

Education being a sub-system of the social system can hardly remain unchanged when the society changes or the people change. Change being the only norm in the world, everything is bound to undergo a change. Some change very slowly like the contours of a mountain, some others change slowly like our body and yet some others change very fast, like a house on fire. This has exactly happened with our system of education. Certain things have changed very fast with unimaginable speed, e.g. mode of communication, while some others have changed slowly like our habits and mind-set and yet others very slowly like some administrators, teachers with very fixed and rigid ideas. Will we now not accept the fact that since change is bound to come in any case, it is wise to accept it willfully, not willy-nilly? In case of a wilful acceptance of the change, education can always give a meaningful direction to the society. Change is like a double-edged weapon cutting both the sides. It is not necessary that change is always for the better or good and meaningful. It can equally be meaningless, harmful and disastrous too. Let us seek answers to the following perplexing questions:

- Why should one change?
- Is change essential? Are all changes always good?
- Can one remain unchanged amidst the changing world?
- Is teaching ethics through computers possible?
- Which are the areas that are fast changing?
- What are priority areas in education which require immediate change?

- What are the areas in education where changes can be delayed? For how long?
- Can older teachers really change like the younger ones?
- Who should be the models of change—the young or the old?
- Why changing technology/method in a class is far easier than changing the teacher?
- How to decide the good and bad aspects of change?
- What should be the pace of change for a student/ teacher?
- Why administrators do not change/modify their approach?
- Should change be imposed on others?
- How to accept change as natural?
- Why politicians change faster than teachers?

We may like to note a few emerging concepts of education as follows:

- Computer Assisted Instruction (CAI).
- Distance-Learning.
- On-line Learning.
- Individualized Instruction.
- De-schooling Society.
- Human Rights Education.
- Value Education.
- Information Technology.
- Countrywide Classroom.
- Virtual Classroom.
- Gyan Darshan.
- Environmental Education.
- Education for Aged.
- Population Education.
- Special Education.
- Adolescent Education.
- Aids Education.
- Family Life Education.

- Lifelong Education.
- Open Learning Education.

When all these emerging concepts are incorporated into the domain of education and analyzed thereof, education appears to be responsive to the pressing needs of the time. Education to be an elixir of life needs to be always a dynamic and vibrant process of the present, taking care of the future but without missing the goodness of the past. It needs to train the minds of the millions. It must break the age-old inertia of the society in terms of its dogmas, blind-beliefs, superstitions and unscientific practices. It doubly needs to train their minds so as to remain composed amidst sudden and violent changes.

Dimensions of Education in the Twenty-First Century

As we advance into twenty-first century, we happen to encounter a number of things which we could hardly have ever imagined. After the amazing breakthroughs in the areas of communication technology, it is now quite clear that, we are living in a shrinking world and are undergoing the transition to a global society. It appears as if the era of the world being a single family (*Vasudhaiva Kutumbkam*) is just on the anvil. As the new century opens the vistas of newer possibilities almost in every field, say in health, medicine, commerce, communication, infrastructures, science and technology, engineering, law, agriculture, defence, etc. so also it poses equally serious challenges alongside. After obtaining unprecedented achievements in medical science, i.e. control over diseases, the scientists are engaged seriously in human cloning and even taking up the challenges to defy death as our necessary predicament. The big question here is, what about its ethical dimension? Who is going to decide the desirability or undesirability of such probing and how? Let us, for our convenience, identify few salient features of the twenty-first century as under:

- Globalization.
- Personalization.
- Interdependence.
- Faster communication.
- Cultural transition/conflicts.

- Environmental/Ecological concerns.
- Changing values/priorities.
- e-commerce, e-governance.
- Wider accessibility/New knowledge.
- Revolution in Communication Technology.

The Possibilities and Challenges

Let us look at the Table 2.3 for a synoptic view of the contrasting position of the new century in terms of its possibilities and challenges:

Table 2.3: Possibilities and Challenges of New Century

Possibilities	Challenges
Shrinking geographical boundaries	Increasing International tensions/ conflicts
Greater individual independence	Greater interdependence among the nations
Faster communication	Slower understanding
Cultural assimilation	Loss of identity
Availability/arrival of new medicines/health care facilities	Negligence of age-old practices/health rules
Changing value systems	Conservative value system
Growing awareness about human rights	Misuse of power in oppressing people
Growing materialism	Losing spirituality
Getting global	Loosing sight of the individual/local
Unbounded flexibility	Lack of perspectives

We may also like to identify more and more possibilities by listing the challenges alongside for advancing our comprehension of the new century.

Since the new century does not arrive with sky-high promises alone and at every step it also poses great challenges, the need of the hour is to know how to meet these challenges. Education is the potent changing force of society. Thus, there are great expectations of the society from the teachers. The visionaries pin their hopes in education, tender the upcoming generations organically fit and mentally well-equipped in tackling the demands of the new century with ease and competence.

Table 2.4 will give an idea of the emerging areas and the inputs required in these areas so as to facilitate the impending changes in the society.

Table 2.4: Emerging Areas in the Society

Dimensions	Inputs Required
Universal/Global concerns	Education for all, Human rights, Equality of opportunities, Universal entry, Universal retention and universal exit (Universalization of Education), Functional literacy, Open learning, Lifelong education, Virtual institutions
Individual/Personal	Freedom of choice, Self-learning with individual pace, Time, Style, Learner-centered education, Individualized instruction, Experiential learning
Socio-Cultural	Openness, Flexibility, Cultural assimilation, Participatory, Democracy, Social-justice, Ethnicity or cultural identity, Contextuali-zation, Mutuality, Communal harmony
Economic	Productivity (growth), Development, Sustainability, Gainful employment. Free markets, E-commerce, Competition, Co-operatives, Autonomy, Reduction, Mitigation of hunger, Disease, Death, Poverty and malnutrition, Privatization, Multinationals, Consumerism
Political	Global citizenship, International understanding International laws, Legislation, Judiciary
Techno-Professional Information	Technologies, Computers, Internet, Websites, Transparency, Technical know-how, Skill, Competency, Mass-media, Multi-media, Super-specialization, Inter-disciplinary tendencies, Integration, Need for regular upgradation of knowledge
Environmental	Ecological safer, Sustainable development, Pollution control mechanism, Deforestation, Respect for all forms of life, stakeholders

Education, if not to be an unexciting experience and routine job, must plunge in and dynamically respond to the dynamic society. It must prepare new teachers, unlike past, with new values, commitments and competencies. The contents and processes of education must be readjusted and reformulated.

With an in-built flexibility of accommodating temporal changes in the society, the modes and methods of curriculum transaction must quickly adopt the information technology like computers, multi-media, mass media, internet, web-sites, etc. for greater, wider and lasting impact. A teacher supported by technology is definitely more empowered than an effective teacher who is without such support.

The UNESCO International Commission on Education for the Twenty-first Century's Report (J. Delros) on 'Learning—the treasure within' envisages the four pillars of education as under:

- Learning to Know.
- Learning to Do.
- Learning to Be.
- Learning to Live Together.

As regard to the fourth pillar of education, i.e. learning to live together, the very intent of education is to develop a citizenry which will essentially learn the value of mutual respect and interdependence thereof. Man being a social being does not and need not learn how to live alone. Rather the very social nature of him acknowledges the very existence of other members of the society and presupposes the meaningful interaction with them by allowing mutual adjustments. The demand of the new millennium is meaningful interaction amongst nations for greater co-operation and mutual development.

Learning—The Treasure Within: Science and Art of Living

The International Commission on Education has rightfully christened the title of its report "Learning the Treasure within". In fact, learning is really a treasure. It is really most valuable treasure for man. There is no treasure over and above learning. If 'knowledge is power', as Francis Bacon said, "Learning is the most empowering experience". If 'Ideas rule the world', learning is the golden path to the kingdom of ideas and the ultimate ruler of the world. Learning being a stimulating experience is more an internal process than an external one. It is very much in tune with the ideas of Swami Vivekanada and Mahatama Gandhi on education, that is, "Education is the manifestation of divine perfection already in man" and "Education is the drawing out of the best in child and man-body, mind and spirit".

Learning as Science and Art of Living

Learning, instead of being either science or art of living is infact, both of these. Observe Table 2.5 and find out, how it is so?

Table 2.5: Learning as Science and Art

Learning As

Science	*Art*
Systematic	Individual
Rational	Stylish/Typical
Empirical	Creative
Experimental	Performance-based
Objective	Appreciative
Logistic	Novel
	Aesthetic
	Joyful experience/self-Satisfying
	Enlightening/Refreshing
	Energizing
	Emotive
	Expressive

The contents of the Table 2.5 reveal that learning is a systematic and step-by-step endeavor. It is patterned and follows some rational principles. Besides, learning is basically a personal act involving unique experience in the process of entering the environment. It arises out of the needs of the learner acquired and terminates in self-satisfaction. The learning is internalized and practically applied in various situations of life. It is in a way typical to the individual, thereby giving an artistic touch to the entire process of learning.

Learning can also be a means as well as an end. As we grow in years and live different stages of life (i.e. infancy, childhood, adolescent, adult) and encounter various situations we learn many things. Here, learning becomes an end and outcome of living. Learning as a means enriches our life continuously. As we learn, so we better adjust and accommodate in difficult situations. Learning also helps us in improving continuously the quality of life and living. Learning takes us to the essence of life. With learning and education we reach the unreached. Thus, it becomes both a science as well an art of living.

Role of Teacher in Emerging Global Society

As everything around changes so do our concepts of students, schools, library, society, technology, value system, culture, economy, politics, religion, authority and administration undergo change. How can the teacher and consequently his/her role remain static? Delineating role of a teacher in the context of an emerging global society is not an easy task. The role of teachers is always subject to the goals of education and the types of society with its dominant ideology. In an authoritarian system the teachers are supposed to function in a distinctly different manner than in a democratic society. What is expected of a teacher is also relative to the time period, place and people. We can have a quick look at the changing roles of teachers over time as given in Table 2.6.

Table 2.6: Changing Roles of Teachers

Period	Role of Teacher
Ancient	Authoritative, Parental, Personal, Reflective, Perspective, Guiding
Medieval	Dogmatic, Ritualistic, Disciplinarian, Metaphysical, Super-intendent
Modern	Analytic, Impersonal, Suggestive, Associative/ Friendly, Helping, Competent, Specialized

Contd...

Contd...

Period	Role of Teacher
Post-Modern Emerging	Speculative, Participatory, Collaborative, Transactive, Excellency, Super-specialized, Sensitive to individuals needs

Emerging Role of Teacher

Considering the magnitude and pace of change in twenty-first century, it becomes imperative for the system of education, as well as for the teacher, to understand, accommodate and give a direction to change, wherever possible. Among all agents of change, the teacher has got the most vital and responsible role to play. He/She is considered as the path breaker or harbinger of change. The present time demands that the teachers perform some of the following roles:

Pro-active Role of Teacher

When the winds of change come, the teacher should not remain as a mute and passive spectator. By doing so, we can neither stop the change nor give it any desirable direction. It would rather be wise for a teacher to understand why and how the 'change' occurs in the society. The teacher meaningfully participates in the process of social change. By doing so, a teacher not only keeps himself/herself active but also grows in experience (learning by doing) and helps in advancing the cause of progress.

Managerial Role of Teacher

The image and the role of a teacher, as traditionally perceived, is the most revered 'Guru' (Master). He is a strict 'disciplinarian' and is considered as the most learned/wise person in the society in this fast changing world. The conventional faith that teachers 'are born" is being replaced by the practice—teachers are made. Since the nature of future society is going to be drastically different, the role of teacher is also likely to be different.

The teacher is expected to be a good and efficient manager of learning resources. His management skills of providing information to the students, identifying learning needs of pupils and also resources and ability of creating a "learning base" is gradually becoming much more important than his 'character role' or 'teaching competency'. A multi-cultural society will have multi-natured students with unequal levels, expectations, and personality profiles. The major challenge before the teacher is how to manage these resources together with equal level of satisfaction.

The learning process is becoming personalized/individualized. It demands a teacher to make a real "need-assessment" of all pupils and adopt differential management strategies. The teacher may take advantage of modern technology like computers, e-mail, internet/websites, multiple community resource, etc. For managing the demands of children and community, a teacher needs to manage himself/herself first. This may be called self-management of the teacher. In order to become the best type of manager and obtain the optimum out-put, a teacher needs to rationally plan out his/her time, energy and resources for meaningful utilization.

Socio-cultural Role of Teacher

A teacher being a true representative of a particular society and culture has got a responsible role to play for both. The teacher is always a social reformer. Great educators have been great social reformers. For any reformation, the society always looks towards a teacher more than any one else. Such expectation of the society makes a teacher more accountable for the removal of existing dogmas, blind-beliefs, superstitious practices and inculcation of scientific temper in the society. An emerging teacher is required to become a role-model for students, family members, children and others by not being a follower of dowry system, casteism, racism, religious intolerance, sex-biases, rigidity, child-marriage, practices of *Sati*, etc. Rather he/she should question and help to demolish them.

History and Development of Indian Education

3

In order to understand the history of education of a country, it is very necessary to comprehend on various factors, currents and cross-currents which effect the onward march. And of all these, civilization and culture play a very dominant role. They are closely associated, rather inter-linked, with education. Anything that causes their rise or decline also has an impact on the growth of education or vice-versa. India is known to be a very ancient country. Indian traditions prove this contention. Even modern-day historians of the world admit that India is one of the most ancient nations with rich legacies of culture and literary pursuits which very few nations can boast of. It has had its own vast reservoir of literatures which, again, proves as to how this country had achieved progress even in those days when many parts of the world were still in the primitive stages.

History of Education in India according to many historians starts with the creation *of Rigveda* which broadly narrates the philosophy of life and the practices in the realm of learning. Thus history of education in India according to modern thinkers is nearly 5000 years old. For a comprehensive and systematic study, it can be classified as follow:

Table 3.1: History of Education in India

• Vedic Era	3000 B.C. to 500 B.C.
• Buddhistic Era	500 B.C. to 1200 A.D.
• Muslim Era	1200 A.D. to 1700 A.D.
• British Era (the Pre-Independence Era)	1800 A.D. to 1947
• Post-Independence Era	1947 onwards

Education in Ancient India

India is a very ancient country. It has a very rich, social, cultural and philosophical heritage. The rich traditions of this country have attained the status of legends. The ocean of literatures is unfathomable. The Vedas are regarded as the oldest among the literatures of the world. The Vedas are not only the original source of philosophy of life in this part of the sub-continent since times immemorial but also of the system of education in ancient India.

Vedic Education

As for the derivation of the word *Veda*, it is found in the four roots, viz. *"Vid Sattaym", "Vid Labhe", "Vid Vichare"* and *"Vid Gyane"*. Generally speaking, the word *Veda* means "to know". This meaning has deeper implications. Knowledge did not mean merely the knowing of some literatures in the general sense of the term but it connoted knowledge of oneself, knowledge of universe, knowledge of 'Bramha' or God. The meaning thus had very wide philosophical ramifications. Vedas have not only been the repositories of spiritual knowledge, but also embody in themselves the sublime, religious feeling of human beings as well as the foundational knowledge of the manifesto universe. Aspects of Indian life are represented by four Vedas, viz. *Rigveda, Yajurveda, Atharvaveda,* and *Samveda.* They also represent religions, materialistic, conjugal and spiritual instincts and pursuits through *brahmacharya*, *grihastha*, *vanprastha* and *sanyas ashrams*. Hence the Vedas are not merely the books of Philosophies or knowledge but the books of life.

The Vedas denote a graphic account of education. What an individual should know and what not is the essence of education for life. That is why, it laid down four Ashrams of life. The Vedas have also planned out the four levels of existence, viz. of knowledge of action, of devotion, and of wisdom for an ardent seeker of knowledge. Education of a beginner could only commence after the thread ceremony of or *Upnayan Sanskar,* conferring him the status of "'Dwij' or Dwijanma". This ceremony symbolises the entrance of an individual to the new or the second life in the pursuit of 'gyan' or knowledge through the *Brahmacharya Vrata*—life of celibacy. On this occasion, the preceptor declares him, "Thou art a Brahmachari" and explains him the supreme goal of life to realize one's identity with 'Brahma'—the ultimate and the divine source of this universe. The preceptor also explains that knowledge (*gyan*), action (*karma*) and devotion (*bhakti*) are the means of realising the ultimate objective. The 'Brahmachari' or the celibate would bid farewell to his home and reside in the hermit/*ashram*/*kuti* of his preceptor. By renouncing worldly and material pleasures and comforts of life, he would gradually realize that the only reality is the "Brahma" and the rest or the world is just an illusion.

Vedas lay great stress on action (*karma*) which decides the destiny. The doctrine of '*karma*' occupies an important place in the Indian system of life. According to the Vedic philosophy, "Karmas" (Actions) should lead to the ultimate objective of attaining salvation (moksha), i.e. the union of 'Atma' with 'Parmatma'. It also means that the 'karma' should not lead an individual to attaining materialistic happiness or instincts but its main aim should be to keep him free from worldly bondages. Education, according to this philosophy, makes an individual judicious, highly spiritual and unattached to greed, lust for attaining the high degree of individuality. The preceptor leads him to meditation and 'tapas' (Penance).

Thus the philosophy is built upon the tenets of spirituality which is the corner stone of the ancient system of education. The main characteristic of ancient Indian education is the inculcation of the spirit of plain living and high thinking, of brotherhood, (*Vasudhaiva Kutumbakam*) and constant awareness of the omni-presence and omni-science of the 'Brahma' (God). The ancient system of education lays great stress on strict adherence to various aspects of life, a high degree of moral and spiritual values. Ideal ways of life emanated from the actual living of the preceptor under whose feet the 'Brahmachari' or the pupil learnt the lessons.

The Guru lived in his hermit in a solitary place on the bank of a river or near the mountains away from the maddening crowd and worldly strifes. The vicinity provided an ideal setting for learning through meditation and rigorous 'Tapas'. It is through the nature's bountiful environment that the pupil learn to discard ignoble thoughts and deeds. In such an environment the pupil could learn the first lessons of duty, devotion, dedication and discipline. The life of the Gurus used to be the role model for his disciples. He was an ideal Guru in the real sense of the term.

VEDIC ERA

In the preceding paragraphs, it has been made amply clear that the 'Vedas' were the real source of Indian philosophy and education. Rightly it is, therefore, called the Vedic era in the history of Indian education. We have already seen that the Vedas symbolized the chief objective of human life—the deliverance from the world of births and deaths and reunion with the supreme power. Hence the main aim of education during the era has been the attainment of this goal. The other aims of education may be short listed in the following words:

Aims of Education

- To ensure the preservation of the rich legacies of the Vedas, Vedic literature, Vedic rituals and also ensure their smooth transition to the next generations,
- To ensure strict adherence to Vedic rituals and ways of life and to strive for the enrichment of Vedic traditions,
- To enable to lead one's life in accordance with the Vedic philosophy of life in which spiritual values and moral principles should be the sheet-anchor, and
- To ensure an all-round development of personality—physical, mental, moral and spiritual.

Gurukulas

The system of education during this period revolved round the Gurukulas. The Gurukulas were the centres of learning. The hermits or the abodes of the sages and saints were known as Gurukulas where the pupils also resided with their gurus and lived an austere life after leaving their homes. The Gurukulas, also known as Rishikulas were situated in isolated and lonely places far away from the crowded localities or townships, on the banks of rivers or amidst the woods, the natural settings provided an ideal environment for pursuing learning. There was no distinction between the rich and the poor, the royals and the downtrodden. The Gurukulas did not depend upon the benedictions of the State, they were free from their control. They depended on their own resources.

The Gurukulas were not only the covetted seats of learning but also of great "Yajnas". Gurus enjoyed a unique position in the society. They used to be the most revered persons. They were immensely respected not only from their disciples but also from the entire society, even the kings bowed their heads before them and sought their wise counsel. They enjoyed this status due to their sharp intellect, chaste character, high morals and great wisdom.

Upnayan Ceremony

The pupil was admitted in the Gurukula only after the initial sacred ceremony of 'Upnayan'. The ceremony had a great importance from education point of view, for the teacher used to purify his physical self for the new enlightened body. After this ceremony, the pupil was entitled to receive learning.

The word 'Upnayan' means, "to come" close. In the context of education this word signifies that the student should come near the teacher for receiving education. Later on this ceremony became very important for Brahmins. On this occasion the Guru used to give him his "Mantras". In *Atharvaveda*, we find elaborate description of the *sanskar*. The teacher used to decide the kind of education to be given to him after keeping him close for three days. In vedic tradition, human life was divided into four ashrams—viz. *brahmacharya*, *grihastha*, *vanprastha* and *sanyas*.

Antewasi

During the period of stay in the Gurukula the pupil was known as "Antewasi" or "Acharyakulavasi". At the time of his induction, in the gurukula, he was instructed with a number of "do's and dont's" by the teacher. These are elaborately scripted in '*Gobhil guhya/sutras*'. The daily routine prescribed for the student was well organized and life in the Gurukulas was disciplined and orderly.

Curriculum

Various subjects formed part of the curriculum such as grammar, rhetorics, astrology, logic, nirukti (etymological interpretation of words) and *kalp*. The study of the Vedas was compulsory. Upanishads, Sutras and Samhitas also formed part of curriculum. These elaborate rules for the construction of altar led to the development of the sequences of geometry and algebra. The desire to find out propitious times gave rise to astrology, from which astronomy developed.

Methods of Teaching

There were mostly two methods of teaching practised during this period. The first was oral and the other was 'chintan' (thinking or reflecting). Oral method means memorisation of Vedic hymns, mantras, richas and slokas, the various lines of the verses, with correct pronunciation and meanings. The success of the method lies on the fact that the Vedas, their mantras and richas could be preserved in their original form down to the ages. Thinking was another method which promoted self-understanding and self-confidence. Thinking led to 'manan'—a high form of thinking. Through this, the meaning and implications or the 'mantras' were further developed, elaborated and preserved in one's own mind. This method of teaching was specially adopted for highly intelligent students.

Place of Women

During the Vedic age, women enjoyed equal status with men not only in education but also in social, religious and other programmes as well. Education of women during this period was at its peak. There had been many eminent women during this era who enjoyed important place in the society. Women like Ganga, Lopa Mudra, Apala Ghosh, Sita and Vishwara were some examples.

Place of Teacher

The teacher (Guru, Acharya) enjoyed a very predominant place during this period and the later post-vedic periods not only in his Gurukul but also in the entire society. Every one looked up to him for guidance and blessings. He was a friend, philosopher and guide in the real sense. The relationship between the teacher and the pupil was ideal and cordial. The Guru was the protector of his students and in turn students accorded more respect to him than even to their father. The teacher shouldered the responsibility of the students during the period of his study in the Gurukulas.

Daily Routine of Student

The student had to adhere to the Gurukul rules of discipline, punctuality and conduct. No discrimination was made in this regard between students. Observance of celibacy, performance of daily sacred rituals like yoga, meditation, yajna recitation of vedic richas were an inseparable aspect of education. Besides this, practical education formed an integral part of the system, viz. collecting fire woods for yajna-kundas, begging alms and looking after the cattle. Students were also supposed to help the Guru and his wife in daily and domestic chores.

Duration of Education

There was no fixed or rigid duration of education. It depended solely on the caliber and desire of the students to pursue their education and also on the Guru who had the final say in the continuance or discontinuance of the students education. There are examples of students who continued to stay in the Ashrams for an indefinite period. But in most other cases the duration was of twelve years. There used to be holidays, known as 'Anadhyay'. These were given on the important festivals or on days like Ashtmi, Chaturdashi and at times of natural disasters like heavy rains and floods.

BUDDHIST ERA

In the post-Vedic age, though the system of education of ancient times continued to hold its ground steadfastly, some of its features started showing signs of decline. In the Vedic period, people started giving place to Brahmanic religion. The caste system spread its vicious influence leading to discrimination in education. Yajnas became the main activities of Gurukulas and Ashrams besides education. Violence, both human and inhuman, became the order of the day. In the name of 'Karma-kand' or 'Yajnas' many excesses were committed. Under these conditions there was a need of reforms. The society found its reformer in Lord Buddha who propounded, founded and propagated the real and the time meaning of life. His sayings rapidly overlook the sub-continent.

The teachings of Gautam Budha gave birth to the Budhistic philosophy of life and education. Siddharth, as he was known, was upset and much distressed right from early age to see people in the old age, deaths and sufferings. He renounced his comforts and took to penance for years and was in search of the ways to get rid of griefs and sufferings. Ultimately he got enlightenment.

Monasteries

Budhist movement led to the establishment of Monasteries known as Viharas and Maths. His disciples lived in them. These institutions functioned on democratic lines and were open to all without any discrimination of caste and even sex. The inmates in these monasteries were called 'Bhikshus' (males) and 'Bhikshunis' (females). They led a simple and austere life under the supervision of Gurus.

Monasteries became the centres of learning during this period. Only Bhikshus and Bhikshunis could get education here. There was no place for Yajnas or religious rituals as it was prevalent in the Vedic period.

Pabbajja Ceremony

Admission in these Monasteries was given to a prospective disciple only after going through certain formalities. For admission the student was to present himself before the teacher and request him for giving education. After the teacher's willingness to admit a student in the Monastery, he had to go through an initiation ceremony called *'Pabbajja'*. Pabbajja was an accepted and important ceremony of admission in the Monastery. 'Pabbajja' meant 'going out'. According to this ceremony the student has to renounce all his worldly and family relationships. The minimum age for admission was eight years. After this ceremony, he had to change his clothes and old style of living. For this ceremony, he had to get his head clean shaved and put on yellow robes. Then he would bow before the Guru (Bhikshu) and pray to him for admission. He would recite as follows:

- "I take refuge in Buddha" (*Budhham Sharanam Gachhami*)
- "I take refuge in religion" (*Dharmam Sharanam Gachhami*)
- "I take refuge in the order" (*Sangham Sharanam Gachhami*)

After his admission he was called 'Shraman'. He was given few, advices to follow, such as speaking truth, shunning violence, preaching non-violence and celibacy, renouncing wealth and comfortable life. Admission was not given to those who were suffering from tuberculosis, leprosy and contagious diseases. Parent's consent was necessary for admission.

Upsampda Ceremony

During the Vedic and the post-Vedic periods the students, after the completion of education, could join their families and lead grihastha ashram but under this system a 'Sharaman' after 12 years of education or at the age of 20 years had to undergo another ceremony, the Upsampda Ceremony. This ceremony was different from the 'Pabbajja'. After 12 years of education, the Shraman had to present himself before all other Monks. Ceremony was performed to declare him complete monk. This symbolized the end of his relation completely with his family and relations. Now he was a monk of the monastery, completely devoted to Buddhism.

Curriculum

The main aim of education in this era was to attain salvation (Moksha). The curriculum was mainly spiritual in nature. The study of religious books on Buddhist religion and the philosophy of Buddha formed an integral part of curriculum. There were two types of curriculum, one for the monks and the other, for common people. The first one included subjects like 'Vinaya, Dhamma and Suttanta'. The second one included subjects like spinning, weaving, printing, medicine, surgery and accountancy.

Methods of Teaching

Methods of teaching were not very different from the Vedic age but special emphasis was laid on personal purity and probity of conduct. During the lectures of the teacher, the student was supposed to hear him with rapt attention.

Women education suffered a great setback during this period. During his life time he discouraged their admission in the monasteries. But after some time, women were admitted with many reservations and restrictions. Strict rules were imposed for women Bhikhunis and monks. They were not allowed to meet any male in loneliness. They lived separately from the male counterparts. During this period of education many institutions became very famous not only in India but also in other parts of the world. Buddhism as a religion was propagated and accepted in Sri Lanka, China, Afghanistan, Thailand, Combodia, Vietnam, Japan and flourished there. In many parts of India several dynasties were great followers of Lord Buddha.

FAMOUS CENTRES OF LEARNING IN ANCIENT INDIA

School of Taxila

Takshila was an ancient city in India on the north-west frontier region, now in Pakistan. Even today it is famous with the name of Taxila. It is widely believed that the city was founded by Lord Ram's brother—Bharat's son, Taksha. At that time it was the capital city of Gandhar Kingdom. Although there was no institution on a very organised system, the Acharyas provided education in their hermits on the Vedic pattern and attracted a large number of students from far and wide. Taxila had been the centre of higher learning. Students used to go there for education after 16 years of their age. From the old literature it is found that there were two types of curriculum, literary and scientific. Under the first, religious education on Buddhism was imparted while under the second, eighteen shilps, ayurveda, Military science, agriculture, commerce, medicines, etc. were taught. Emphasis was given on practical training. This centre of learning started to decline from the 5th century onwards. Eminent people like Panini, Jeevak, Kautilya and many others received education in Taxila.

School of Nalanda

Nalanda was also a famous centre of education during the Buddhistic era. It is situated 60 km. from Patna and 10 km from Rajgir in Bihar. Nalanda was the birth place of Lord Buddha's dear discipline Somputta. Emperor Ashoka built a Vihara here. Nalanda became famous as a centre of learning during first century. Acharya Nagarjuna Dev was an Acharya of Nalanda. Many rulers received their education at Nalanda. Rulers from the Gupta dynasty did everything to develop Nalanda into an international institute of learning. Foreigners used to come to Nalanda to receive education. Nalanda University had a huge building, a large hostel fully equipped with kitchens and other facilities. About ten thousand students received education at Nalanda free of cost. The university had two hundred villages as grants from which the expenses were met. Fifteen hundred teachers worked here.

School of Vallabhi

Vallabhi was situated in Kathiawad (Gujarat). It was a famous centre of Buddhistic education. Tsang had described about one hundred Maths here. Vallabhi could be compared with Nalanda. Besides religious education, economics, political science and medicine were taught.

School of Vikramshila

This centre was established in the eighth century. King Sharanpat had built a large Vihara at Vikramshila which was the centre of education. Deepshanker was the famous teacher of Vikramshila. Curriculum consisted of education on Buddhism, Vyakarana, Philosophy, Logic, Astrology. Many books of Pali and Sanskrit were translated here in Tibetan language. This great institution was destroyed by Bakhtiar Khilji. Other centres of learning were Kashi, Ujjayini, Amravati, Mithila, Odantpuri and Kanchi. It is thus evident from the above description that the ancient system of education in India had deep roots. That is why it survived and continued for several hundred years. Even the foreigners who visited this country highly acclaimed the merits of the system. These included Megasthnes, Strabo, Huen Tsang, Marco Polo and Ibn Batuta. The principles, ideals and philosophy which ancient Indian system of education followed are still useful today.

EDUCATION IN MEDIEVAL INDIA

A new religion was propounded by Prophet Mohammed called Islam in Arabic. Its followers, known as Muslims, spread it in many parts of the world. India was soon acquainted with this religion after successive Muslim invasions during the medieval period. The first to invade India was Mohd Bin Kasim, an Arab, in 712 A.D. but he could not move beyond Sindh. After this there was no external invasion for about two hundred and seventy five years till the Mughals came and established rule in India.

Muslims were greatly influenced by Indian literature, arts, culture and above all its fabulous wealth. From eleventh century onwards there were spates of external invasions by hordes of Muslim tribes and rulers. Some of them made deep in roads into India and established their dynasties which ruled for a number of years. Among these were the Slave dynasty (1206 A.D. to 1286 A.D.) the Khilji dynasty (1290 A.D. to 1316 A.D.), the Tuglaq dynasty (1322 A.D. to 1389). the Sayyad dynasty (1414 A.D. to 1451), the Lodi dynasty (1451 A.D. to 1526 A.D.) and the Mughal dynasty (1526 A.D. to 1707 A.D.). The Muslims established Mosques, Makbaras and Madarsas for giving education in Islam. In short, external invasions sowed the seeds of Muslim education in medieval India, which took shape under these rulers and depended for its progress mostly on the attitude and enthusiasm of the individual rulers.

Salient Features of Muslim Education

Replacement of Ancient Institutions of Indian Education

When the Muslims invaded and stalled their rule, the system of ancient Indian education was at its peak and a number of institutions attracted the foreigners from far-off countries. Rulers like Bakhtiyar, Mohammed Gazni and Aurangzeb dealt fatal blow to them. They destroyed the old systems and built Maktabs and Madarasas in place of Gurukulas, Ashrams and Maths.

Predominant Place to Persian

Persian foreign language with the State patronage replaced Sanskrit and Pali—the oriental languages of India. Persian became the State language of administration and education. Literature was produced in Persian and Arabic languages.

Education at the Mercy of Rulers

For the first time in the history of Indian education, freedom in the field of education was replaced by the ruler's gross interference, fancies and whims. The rulers had the final say and educational system changed forms from ruler to ruler. This proved to be great setback in the progress of education.

Imparting Education in Mosques

With the establishment of Muslim rule in India, a large number of mosques were built primarily for offering prayers but subsequently they became the place of dissemination of Islamic knowledge.

Religious Bias to Education

Religious education was the core of Muslim education. Strict adherence to the ways of life enshrined in holy Quran formed part of Muslim education. The object of education was to tailor one's life according to Islamic principles.

Organisation of Islamic Education in India

After the establishment of their rule in India, Muslim ruler's agenda was to draw people of other religions to the fold of Islamic religion by preaching or by force. The primary form of education in this era was fully religious. In the early period, education was provided in the mosques but subsequently "Maktabs" were started which were attached to mosques.

Maktabs

Maktabs provided elementary education to children of general public. Children of rich people did not go to the Maktabs, their education was arranged privately in the confines of their homes. The main emphasis in these institutions was to acquaint the children with the verses of holy Quran which was compulsory as an integral part of instruction. Besides, the religious education, they were also taught reading, writing and arithmetic.

The Bismillah Ceremony

Like the Vedic and Buddhist systems, admission in the Maktabs was given only after the first ceremony. On the occasion of admission, the child was taken to the Maktab in new clothes. He was required to repeat some verses of the "Quran". If he could not do this, he was just asked to pronounce "Bismillah" and thus started his education. The "Bismillah" ceremony heralded his educational career. The ceremony was held when a child was 4 years 4 months, 4 days old. After a few days of this ceremony the child was required to write a few words. At this time, his relatives were invited. Besides reading, writing and arithmetic, the children were also taught Persian literature, grammar, letter-writing and accountancy. Children of the royal families, princes and princesses were taught in palaces by old Moulvis. The curriculum for them consisted of various subjects, like Persian and Arabic literature, political science, law, science, jurisprudence, military science, etc. Practical training in warfare was also imparted.

Madarsas

Maktabs essentially provided elementary education, madarsas were established to give higher education during this period. Madarsas became the centres of higher learning. These institutions subsisted often on the royal benedictions, who gave them lands, jagirs, financial grants, etc. The madarsas were generally well managed. The kings took interest and did not interfere in their working.

The curriculum in madarsas was broad based and catered to various needs. It was religious as well as comprehensive. Under the religious curriculum, intensive study of holy Quran, its philosophy, Islamic history and Islamic law were included. The other parts of the curriculum had subjects like Persian and Arabic literature, their grammar, history, mathematics, geography, Unani medical science, agriculture, philosophy, law, jurisprudence, astrology, economics, accountancy, etc. The period of education was 10 to 12 years. Arabic was generally the medium of instruction, libraries used to be attached with big madarsas. Stress was given on memorising. The students used to memorise verses of holy Quran. Generally, the method of learning was oral, writing work was also done, but there were no scientific methods of teaching. In madarsas lectures were given. Some practical training was also imparted. There was no formal examination system as such. The Moulvis or Mullahs who were generally the teachers decided as to whether the student was competent to go ahead. They had their own method of assessing the capacity of the student. They used to be examined form time to time in practical situations of life. Their intelligence was put to test in solving some difficult problems.

Teacher-Pupil Relationship

During the Muslim period also the teachers enjoyed great respect as they were supposed to help pupil in developing their personality. Even the kings respected the teachers. The teachers enjoyed complete obedience of their pupils, hence their relations were very cordial as during the ancient period. As the number of students was not very large, it was easy for the teacher to know each and every student very well. This solved many unknown situations and problems of indiscipline or disobedience. The teacher had immense power to punish indisciplined students. But good students used to be rewarded also.

Women Education

Women were not supposed to come out of their homes uncovered. They had to cover themselves from head to toe. Purdah system has been a part of Muslim culture. During the Muslim rule, it was very strictly and rather ruthlessly imposed. Hence, girls particularly grown ups were not allowed to attend madarsas. However, they were permitted to go to maktabs. During the Muslim period, a large section of the Muslim women population remained without education. Higher education for women was a rare experience. Some exceptions were there. Princesses and women folk or rich and well-to-do people received their education in their homes. Women like Razia Sultan, Princess Gul Badan (daughter of Babar), Zebunissa, Noorjehan and Mumtaz Mahal were not only noted women of their times but also they earned their place in history by dint of their contributions in several fields. But such women were very few in number.

Development of Literature and Arts

Muslim literature made great progress during this period. Later on Arts became a part of educational curriculum. Similarly, the era saw rapid strides in art and architecture, designing, painting, drawing, etc. These also found their place in education during this period. Mughal rulers encouraged the study of arts in education and encouraged the artists.

Military Training

Military training formed a very important part of Muslim system of education. The main objective of Muslim rulers in India was to expand territories of their rule, which required to fight battles. Training in warfare to them was essential to keep the kingdom safe as well as annexing other kingdoms. It is no secret that Muslim rulers established their rule in India due to their supremacy in warfare skills and military prowess. The armed forces required new equipment and military training. Muslim rulers placed great emphasis on this aspect of education.

ROLE OF THE STATE

Education during the Vedic and Buddhist periods were completely independent in every respect. The state had no role to play and exercised no control. Unlike these, the Muslim system of education enjoyed the patronage of the state. Muslim rule was generally monarchical; hence the monarchs exercised immense control on the system. There were instances of educational progress only when the rule was stable and if it was unstable, education suffered much. Rulers of Slave dynasty like Iltuutmish, Razia Sultan and Balban took keen interest in education and built madarsas. Similarly, the founder of Khilji dynasty, Jalaluddin was interested in the development of education, so were some rulers of Tughlaq dynasty.

Muslim education made great strides during the reign of Mughal dynasty, as almost all the rulers were dedicated to the cause of education. Akbar the great left an infallible impression in the field of education by propounding harmonious relationship between Hindu and Muslim cultures. He laid stress on secular system of education. Many institutions of repute were established during the Mughal reign. Centres of learning at Agra, Delhi, Jaunpur, Beedar, Golkunda, Rampur, Lahore, Sialkot, Hyderabad, Ahmedabad and Luknow were some of the examples. Jaunpur was regarded as a very important centre of Muslim learning. It was also known as "Shiraz-e-Hind".

EDUCATION IN PRE-INDEPENDENCE INDIA

Mughal Empire started crumbling in the post-Aurangzeb period. The weak political administration gave way to anarchy, tyranny, misrule and instability. In such prevailing conditions, Europeans came to India. First, primarily with trading interests, they established their companies. Among the visiting Europeans, the British were very clever. They successfully exploited the situation in their favour and meddled in Indian politics only to establish themselves firmly. They established the East India Company which was originally a trading company. During this period of transition, the Indian systems of education, viz. the Vedic and the Buddhist and the Muslim existed but they were decaying due to constant instability and anarchy. The British described the Indian system as "indigenous system of education". Instead of lending it a helping hand they did every thing possible thing to allow it to die. In order to gain political sympathies of the local populace. "The Calcutta Madarsa" (1780) for Muslims and the "Benaras Sanskrit Vidyalaya" (1791) for Hindus were established.

The Charter of 1813

Their design to dabble in the Indian education field became clear from Charles Grant's famous essay "Observation". He described the prevailing Indian educational scene as deplorable and emphasized the need for reforms. The East India company's charter of 1813 paved the way for the British education in India by the company's charter placing rupees one lakh for the reconstruction of literature. The charter of 1813 created a bitter controversy known as "the occidental-oriental controversy" in the history of Indian Education. Protagonists of both the sides stuck to their guns. Oriental view was in favour of old Indian system of education and wanted to develop and enrich Indian literature through Indian languages. The advocates of this view were Warren Hastings, H.T. Princep, Lord Minto, H.H. Wilson, etc. The Occidental view ridiculed the Indian system, its literature and its languages, Lord Macaulay, who played important role in resolving this controversy, was very bitter and sarcastic. About the Indian literature, he said, "A single shelf of European library was worth the native literature of India". He also ridiculed Indian religions, its practices, ultimately, Lord Macaulay's views (which were made clear in his famous minutes known as Macaulay's Minutes) prevailed.

Downward Filtration Theory

Thus, the ground for the British system of education was laid. The British were not primarily interested in the education of masses and, therefore, they propounded the theory of "Downward filtration" in education. Only the Indian elite or top class people would be educated and through them the lower class would also be benefited. The masses will follow the elite gradually and education will reach down to common citizens.

Wood's Despatch of 1854

Charles Wood was then the Chairman of the Board of control of the Company. A charter was issued on July 19, 1854. Charles Wood was the main architect of this despatch of education. Hence, it is known as Wood's Despatch of 1854. This despatch_was a landmark in the education of India. Many things in education even today, owe their genesis to it.

A brief summary of the main recommendations of this despatch are listed below:

Aim of Education

The aim of education was to develop a man with useful knowledge to raise his intellectual, moral and economic status. He should be given such an education which would be useful for the government.

Curriculum

The curriculum should consist of Sanskrit, Arabic and Persian along with English, Western Literature, Science and Law.

Medium of Instruction

It should be English alongside with Indian languages, which are necessary for education of the masses.

Department of Public Instructions

Setting up of Department of Public Instructions in every state with the Director, as its head was a very important recommendation.

University Education

To establish two universities of Calcutta and Bombay was also recommended. The organisation of administration was to be modelled on the pattern of London University.

Graded Education

The despatch recommended the importance of graded education. With this recommendation a well structured system of education came into existence.

System of Grant-in-aid

This recommendation had a far-reaching impact in the field of education. The main purpose of this recommendation was to encourage private and individual efforts in education. Expansion of education could not be done by the Government and hence other philanthropic, non-government organisations were required to come in the field. By a systematic grant-in-aid regime, different kinds of institutions could provide education besides the Government.

Teachers Training

This recommendation led to the establishment of Training Colleges, Training schools (Normal schools) for teachers of different categories. Prior to this there was no arrangement for training of teachers. It was not realised before this recommendation that the teachers also needed well organised training in the art of teaching.

The despatch also made recommendations for the expansion of general women's education, vocational education and publication of books in Indian languages. The despatch according to many educationists and historians is the 'Magna Carta' of Indian Education. For the first time, a well organised, structured and graded system of education and administration came into existence. The process of institutionalisation of education also began. Sir Philip Hartog made this point when he said, "As a result of Wood's despatch, an educational policy was evolved as a part of general policy of Government of India in the interest of India and to develop her intellectual resources to the utmost for her own benefits". The despatch was undoubtedly the main important document of Indian education policy, which had far-reaching impact. A new era in education began with this.

The Indian Education Commission, 1882

After the Wood's Despatch the country rose against the British empire in 1857 as a sequel to the transfer of power from the Company to the British Monarch. At many places the British faced the wrath of the people but the mighty empire quelled the revolt. By 1882 it was thought necessary to assess the development of education in the country and to remove defects, a commission of education was set up under the chairmanship of Willaim Hunter on February 3, 1882. Besides him, there were other twenty members in the commission. It is also known as the *'Hunter Commission of Education, 1882'*. Among other things the main purpose of the commission was to study the problem of primary education and to suggest remedial measures for the reform. It was also asked to assess the utility of the grant-in-aid system. The Commission chose to study the affairs of secondary and higher education also. It submitted a voluminous report consisting of 700 pages. The main recommendations of the commission are summarised below:

Primary Education

It stressed on the importance of primary education. It should be related to life, practical and useful. Medium of instruction should be the mother tongue of the students. The Government should give more attention to primary education.

But the management of primary education should be entrusted to local bodies, such as District Board, Municipalities in town areas.

Primary school teachers should be suitably trained. Normal schools should be established for their training.

Secondary Education

The commission recommended that the responsibility of Secondary education should be entrusted to the Indians and it should only give grant-in-aid. Medium of instruction at this level should be English. Its curriculum should be divided into two parts. In the first part, subjects of general education and vocational courses in the second part should be framed.

The Commission also emphasised the training of graduate teachers to improve the teaching standards at the secondary school level. Grant-in-aid should have uniformity throughout the country.

The Commission also made recommendations for strengthening of higher education, Indianisation of resources, women's education and other aspects of education.

The recommendations of the commission have a special place in the history of education. It is worth while to note that it was the first ever commission to look into educational problems. It drew attention to the growing problems of education in the country.

Progress of Education in the 19th Century

Indian systems of education of the Vedic, the Buddhist and the Muslim periods were still surviving within the country when the British people decided to make a break from the prevailing systems. The 19th century saw the end of a bitter controversy between the occidental and oriental points of view. A new system of education was formulated by Wood's despatch of 1854, which gave fillip to the establishment of new institutions. During the early period of 19th century not much progress was noticed except in Madras, Bombay presidencies and also in Bengal. A number of schools started functioning in these areas. In the wake of the recommendations of Wood's despatch many initiatives were taken, notable among them were the establishment of Directorate of public instructions in provinces, evolution of the system of grant-in-aid, establishment of universities, expansion of primary and secondary schools through local efforts, but the problem of finance did not help in the expansion of primary education as desired. Missionaries were working in the field of education from the days of their companies. They were rendering their services in other fields as well. But their policy of proselytisation came in for severe criticism.

In the field of education they established some very good institutions. Political scene had also been volatile and surcharged first due to the first abortive freedom movement in 1857 and secondly due to the formation of Indian National Congress in 1885. Education did not receive priority. Lord Curzon came to India in 1899 as the Viceroy and earnestly endeavoured to improve Indian education.

Indian Universities Act, 1904

It was the effort of Lord Curzon that for the first time the Indian Universities Act was passed in 1904. Some of the important aspects of the Act are detailed below:

- Universities should provide teaching. They should not be merely the examining bodies.
- Number of members and their tenure was fixed.
- The executive power of the university would be vested in the syndicate, which would also have professors.
- Role and power of the Senate were also defined.

The beginning of the 20th century saw the rise of "Swadeshi" movement. This motivated several Indians like Gopal Krishna Gokhale to initiate reforms in education. His demand for reforms in education was presented in the form of a bill before the Government. Demand of reforms in other fields also became strong but the outbreak of the first world war in 1914 made the pace somewhat slow.

The Calcutta University Commission, 1917

The Commission was appointed in 1917 under the chairmanship of Sir M.F. Sadler. It is also known as the Sadler

Commission. Though the purpose of appointment of the Commission was to look into the problems of Calcutta University, it was asked to study the conditions of other universities as well. The main recommendations of the Commission are given below:

- The universities should be given enough freedom and autonomy in their functioning. Its powers should be widened.
- The VCs should be salaried official.
- Courses should be redesigned and honours course should be introduced.
- University court should be more representative. This should make the place of Senate.
- There should be a broad and an academic committee, which would prescribe the curriculum.

The Commission also made recommendations about secondary education, which according to it had several defects. It recommended for admission in colleges and universities only after the Intermediate examinations. The graduate course should be of three year's duration. Board of High school and Intermediate examination should be established in each province. They should function free of Department of Education. The Commission looked into other fields, such as women education, teachers training, vocational education, etc. The recommendations of the Commission served as guidelines for not only Calcutta University but also for other universities. Its recommendation for an independent body for examination at the secondary level was timely and useful. The Commission was criticized also for learning too much on the patterns of Cambridge and Oxford Universities of England for modeling Indian Universities.

Education Under Dyarchy

With the end of the First World War in 1919, the demand for freedom dominated the political scene in the country. In order to assuage Indian feelings, the British government introduced Dyarchy in the British India. Under the dyarchy, some subjects of administration were reserved for the members of the executive council and some were transferred to the elected members. Reserved subjects were important subjects like home, law and order, justice and finance while under the transferred subjects, those subjects were classified which were of public welfare, such as, education, health, local bodies, etc. The reforms proved to be great illusion as no fruitful work could be done due to artificial compartmentalization of administration.

Hartog Committee

Simon Commission was appointed in 1927 to look into the political conditions in the country. This Commission was authorised to appoint a committee on education, so a committee was appointed under Sir Philip Hartog to study the various aspects of education. It submitted its report in 1929. Its recommendations with regard to primary education were very important.

The Committee emphasized the importance of primary education and blamed the provincial governments for its neglect. The main causes of poor progress of primary education were lack of financial support, poor curriculum and standards, lack of local efforts, etc. It pointed out that primary education was receiving setback due to two inherent weaknesses in the system-wastage and stagnation. By wastage it meant the leaving of the school without completing education and by stagnation it meant the retention of a child in a class for more than one year. The other findings of the Committee on primary education are given below:

- University education was progressing at the cost of primary education.
- Most of the areas remain unconnected due to lack of transport and other facilities.
- Superstitious and social beliefs are hindrances to the growth of primary education.
- Need to encourage single teacher schools.
- Lack of proper inspection, guidance and supervision.

The Committee also stated the position of secondary education and found it better than primary education. It also hinted at some of its shortcomings. According to it, the sole purpose of secondary school students was to receive university education. It also found great wastage in secondary education, for a large number of students failed in examinations. It also criticised the secondary school curriculum, which was narrow and failed to help students to stand on their legs after its completion. The Committee had concentrated its attention on primary and secondary education but it also gave some suggestions for higher education. Though it praised the rise in the number of students and institutions in this field, it criticised the lowering of Standards and called for its upgradation.

Provincial Autonomy, 1935

It has already been pointed out that the dyarchy form of Government failed to satisfy the aspirations of the Indian people. Subjugation and repression enthused the people to rise against the British Empire. The Indian National Congress and its several national leaders under the leadership of Mahatma Gandhi spearheaded the revolution for complete independence. This led the government to come forward with constitutional reforms of 1935, known as Provincial Autonomy which removed some of the anomalies of dyarchy. Representative governments of elected members were formed in the provinces but this also coincided with the outbreak of Second World War which hampered the cause of education.

The Abbott-Wood Report, 1937

During this period a two-member team constituted by the then Government of India was invited from Britain to propose a plan for vocational education in the country. In all the previous Government reports it was clearly pointed out that vocational education in India had not made any headway for want of clear plan and perspective. With this, the public also posed their demand for its formation. The two British experts were A. Abbott and S.H. Wood. Within four months of their appointment in 1937, they submitted their report to the Government. Its main recommendations are given below:

- Vocational education should be organised according to the local vocational needs of the areas.

- Vocational education should be treated at par with literary and science education.
- Vocational education should be considered to be complimentary to other forms of education.
- There should be separate schools for vocational education.
- Vocational education Advisory Board should be constituted in each province.
- There should be junior and senior vocational schools. Junior vocational schools after VIIIth with 3 year courses and senior schools with 2 year courses after Xth.
- Vocational schools should be established near vocational centres.
- Certificates should be issued after passing a vocational course.

Sargeant Report on Education

As the Second World War was coming to close and the British became hopeful of their victory, it directed its attention to the reforms in education in India. So it advised Sir John Sargeant, the then Educational Advisor to the Government of India to prepare a scheme of education for Indians. He submitted his scheme in 1944. The scheme is known as the Sargeant Report. It had covered all the stages and suggested reforms for each of them. Some of the important suggestions are listed below:

- Compulsory education should be provided to all boys and girls in the 6-14 age group. This should be divided with juniors 6-11, and seniors 11-14 years of age.
- Pre-primary education should be given to children in 3-6 years age group.
- High school education should be divided into two parts— Literary high school and vocational high school.
- The curriculum for literary high schools should have Indian languages, Mother tongue, English, History,

Geography, Civics, Mathematics, Science, Economics, Agriculture and Music, etc. In the other group applied sciences should be taught along with wood work, metal work, Engineering subjects, short-hand, typing, etc.

- For girls students the report recommended for inclusion of Fine arts, Home Science, etc.
- The report also suggested for the abolition of Intermediate classes.
- To check overcrowding in the universities, the report suggested that only 1% high school passing out students should be selected for pre-university education.
- It recommended for the setting up of University Grant Commission.
- It suggested for the improvement of teachers' economic condition.
- It also recommended for setting up of part-time and full-time schools for teaching technical and professional subjects for in-service and other people.

The report also made recommendations about improvement of health of students.

The report is an acknowledgement of British Government, about its utter failure in education in India. The report was short, but very comprehensive and broad-based with some good and worthwhile suggestions. The Government of India accepted its recommendations in principle and tried to implement them. For the first time a Department of education was set up at the centre. All India Technical Education Committee was also established in Delhi.

DEVELOPMENT IN EDUCATION

The freedom movement had a great impact in the field of education. Many nationalists considered the prevailing system completely alien, harmful and indifferent to Indian interests. A call of boycott led to the establishment of institutions of different variety with emphasis on 'Swadeshi'. During this period some innovative schemes were also launched.

Compulsory Education

The concept of compulsory education had been relatively new in India. Gopal Krishna Gokhale was one of the first among such people who fought for the introduction of compulsory education for school going children. He also prepared and presented a bill in this regard. But 'Sayaji Rao Gaekwad', the ruler of Baroda, princely state was the first pioneer who introduced it in 1897 in Amreli Taluka of his state, which became an example. Compulsory education was finally accepted by the British Government only during the last years of its rule. The Sargeant Report accepted the concept and recommended for its implementation.

Basic Education

In the wake of the constitutional reforms in 1935, the Indian National Congress formed its Governments in several provinces. This provided them with the opportunity to implement some of their own schemes of education. One such scheme was the system of 'Vidya Mandir Schools' in old C.P. and Barer. The father of the scheme was the then Chief Minister Pandit Ravi Shankar Shukla. The scheme was primarily meant for rural education. The other scheme of 'Voluntary Schools' was introduced in the then Bombay Presidency. But the most outstanding was 'Basic Education' propounded by Mahatma Gandhi.

Basic Education scheme is also known as "the Wardha Scheme". Mahatma Gandhi convened a conference of educationists at Wardha on October 22 and 23, 1937 to consider the scheme of Basic Education. A committee was formed under Dr. Zakir Hussain to formulate the working details of the scheme. Within two months, the committee submitted its report. The main features of Basic Education are summarised below:

- Education to be given through handicraft. The main aim of Basic Education is to make the child self reliant to enable him to use skills in later life. Through this, a healthy and direct relationship between knowledge and life would be established.

- Medium of education under this scheme would be the mother-tongue of the child through which he can express himself.
- The child is the centre of education under this scheme. The main aim of education is to develop the all-round personality of the child and the handicraft is the most suitable medium for this. It would develop his body, mind and soul.
- Provision of systematic and organized knowledge to the child is important. The child will gain knowledge of other subjects—History, Geography, Mathematics, Agriculture sciences and trade through the handicraft that he chooses.
- Education to be given in the natural setting. Nothing is to be imposed on the child. Flexible curriculum is another feature of Basic education. However the curriculum would consist of: (a) Basic craft such as, spinning and weaving, carpentry, pottery, leather work, culturing fish, etc., (b) Mother tongue, (c) Mathematics, (d) Social Studies (History, Civics, Geography to be combined), (e) Painting and Music, (f) P.T. Drill and Sports, etc. and (g) General Science.

Training of Teachers

The success of the scheme depended upon teachers who were devoted, dedicated and full of zeal and who understood and believed in its philosophy. Hence special training programmes were organised in Wardha for teachers. The training was of two types:

- One year short duration course.
- Two year long-term training course.

Basic education scheme was implemented in all the provinces ruled by the Congress Governments. The Central Advisory Board of education had appointed a committee under B.G. Kher, the then Chief Minister of Bombay to suggest measures for reorganising Basic Education. Kher committee's suggestions were accepted by the CABE. One of the important changes was the renaming of Basic Education as "Nai Taleem".

Progress of Education in the First Four Decades of the 20th Century

Due to Lord Curzon's interests in education and his efforts, progress was witnessed in education. He tried for both quantitative and qualitative development of education. Due to the persistent demand of people, several provinces enacted laws for introduction of compulsory education but the paucity of finance was the main hurdle in its total implementation. At the close of 1937, the number of Primary Schools rose to 1,92,244 with an enrolment of 1,02,24,288 from 1,84,829 in 1926 with 1,30,27,313 students in the country. In 1947 the number of Primary Schools was 1,67,700.

Secondary Education made satisfactory progress. There were 7530 High Schools in India with 11,06,803 students whereas in 1905 they were only 5124 with 5,90,129 students. In 1947 (after partition) the number of Secondary Schools was 11,907 (including 1733 schools for girls) with 33,53,856 boys and 3,56,125 girls. In the sphere of teachers' training progress was noticed. In 1912 there were only 15 training institutions with 1400 trainees.

There was rapid and steady progress in higher education after the arrival of Lord Curzon in India. In 1887, Allahabad University was established. For three years no new university came into being. But after this gap, new universities were established. They were Mysore University (1916), Patna University (1917), Banaras Hindu University (1916), Aligarh Muslim University, Lucknow University (1920), Dacca University (1920) (Now in Bangladesh), Osmania University (1918). The number of colleges also increased during the periods. Some new Universities are Delhi (1922), Nagpur (1923), Agra (1927), Andhra (1926), Annamalai (1929), Travancore (1937), Utkal (1945), Saugor (1946), Rajasthan (1947) were established in the last leg of British rule. Although a number of Universities were established, the total number of Universities in India at that time was merely 18 for a population of 40 crores. Progress in other fields like vocational education, women's education, education for backward classes, etc. was not very satisfactory. The ray of hope in educational development was provided by the Sargeant report, which reflected some of the aspirations of Indians.

There were definitely certain glaring defects in the British educational system in India, which the British knew very well, yet it continued. Despite the defects, the system rendered great service to the Indian people. It was this system that brought about mass awakening to breathe in a free country. The system did more good than harm. It also acquainted Indians with modern knowledge and sciences. It also helped in awakening and a desire to recapture the ancient glory. It also instilled a sense of nationalism and democratic way of life and above all, the system taught people the art of governance.

EDUCATION IN POST-INDEPENDENCE AND EMERGING INDIA

India became free from the foreign yoke on August 15, 1947 and thus started the crucial journey towards "tryst with destiny". A partitioned, badly battered and shattered nation needed immediate social reconstruction. Education was one of the means for social upliftment.

The University Education Commission, 1947-48

The Commission was appointed under the chairmanship of Dr. S. Radha Krishnan, the eminent philospher and later the President of India. On November 4, 1948 Educational experts from USA and UK along with Indian educational experts were invited to serve on the Commission. It submitted its report within a year. The Commission studied the problems of University education and gave important recommendations with regard to aims of university education, educational standards, teacher training, research, women education, religious, vocational, medical and law education, medium of instruction, curriculum, examination system, students' problems, university administration and finance and rural universities. Its important recommendations are summarised below:

Aims of Education

The aims of university education should be in accordance with the past cultural traditions, the present conditions and future requirements of the country.

- The aim should be to produce able citizens who would shoulder their responsibilities in different fields in the country.
- To preserve and develop the culture and civilization of the country.
- To generate new ideas and discard those which impede growth.
- To provide opportunities for the acquisition of knowledge and skills.
- To educate the mind and the soul.
- To promote innovations and new thinking.
- To instill moral values and sense of discipline.
- To develop the spirit of universal brotherhood.

Teaching Standard

The Commission was anxious to raise the teaching and examination standards at the university level. It recommended for the highly qualified, dedicated and good teachers in the universities who would take up teaching work. It suggested higher scales of pay for different grades of teaching staff. For promoting research in universities, scholars should be awarded stipends and scholarships.

Curriculum

The curriculum should be re-organised. The courses of studies for universities and intermediate colleges should be according to the needs of the new India. The curriculum should not be an end but only the means. There should be a connecting bond between the general, intellectual and vocational education.

Teacher's Training

More emphasis should be given on the practical experiences rather than on theoretical studies. Teachers in these institutions should have enough experience of teaching in schools. Innovative practices and research should be promoted in these institutions.

Engineering and Technology Education

These institutions should be nationalized. It recommended for the establishment of more colleges of engineering. Its curriculum should be diversified to meet the needs of the country. Stress should be given on practical skills and researches.

Women Education

Education of women should be generally similar but special provision should be made for subjects of practical domestic life as well. More institutions should be established with qualified women teachers.

Religious Education

The Commission has dealt at length on religious education. According to the Commission, the religious education should be in accordance with the constitutional provisions. It should also keep in mind the secular nature of the country. The State has no role to play except to protect the interests of all religions. In view of this the Commission has recommended:

- Instructions in institutions should commence with self-mediation.
- Biographies of great religious leaders like Shankaracharya, Buddha, Jesus Christ, Prophet Mohammad, Guru Nanak, Mahavir, should be included for study in the first year, essentials of all the religions should be taught in the second year and essentials of philosophers of all religions and their problems should be taken for critical study in the final year.

Rural Education

India resides in villages. Therefore, rural universities should be established to promote higher education to rural population with an emphasis on rural subjects.

Administration

The Commission deplored the defects in university administration. It recommended that the universities should be brought under the concurrent list under the state control. The

Central Government should have minimum say in the affairs of the universities. It also suggested norms for the appointment of Visitors, Chancellors, Vice-Chancellors, Syndicates, Faculties, Councils, etc. in the universities.

Finance

The Commission stressed the need to improve the financial status of the university. The State Government should shoulder the entire cost of university education. Income-tax concessions should be given to firms and persons who donate to educational institutions. The Commission had a famous statesman, thinker, teacher as a chairman so it is natural that the Commission's recommendations bore the imprint of his experiences and philosophy. The Commission rightly perceived the vainness, inadequancy of university education and gave valuable suggestions to remove them. Some of its recommendations are in line with the constitutional provisions.

Secondary Education Commission, 1952-53

The field of secondary education had been riddled with several problems and many defects had crept in the system for which it had been criticized earlier also. In view of this, the Government of India appointed the Secondary Education Commission under the chairmanship of Dr. A. Laxman Swami Mudaliar. On September 23, 1952, A.N. Basu was appointed as the secretary of the Commission. After studying various problems of secondary education, the Commission submitted its report on August 29, 1953.

Defects in Secondary Education

The Commission has pointed out the following defects in Secondary Education:

- It is not related to life.
- It is narrow and one sided, fails to develop student's total personality.
- It does not develop independent thinking and initiative.
- System of examination does not evaluate the abilities of students completely.

- Curriculum and teaching methods are pedantic, mechanical and do not create interest.
- Inappropriate ratio between teacher and student in a class.
- The unsuitable medium of instruction.

Aims of Secondary Education

Secondary education is an important point of education for a large number of students. It is the most important connecting link between primary and university education but unfortunately it is the weakest link in the chain. Therefore, the Commission has emphasized the need to lay down aims of secondary education clearly so that it may be reformed and strengthened. The following are the aims of secondary education:

- To produce ideal citizens for a democracy like India, fully embedded with strong national and social feelings to enable them to shoulder their civic responsibilities and duties.
- To develop productive capacity in the students. So after completion of secondary education they may contribute towards the national prosperity.
- To develop their physical, mental, social and emotional powers for the total development of their personality.
- To develop a sense of discipline and quality of leadership in them.

Duration of Secondary Education

According to the Commission, secondary education should given between 11 and 17 years of age which would include three years of junior high school stage and four years of high school stage. Intermediate stage should be abolished by adding one year in secondary education. Thus, the degree course should be of three years duration.

Multipurpose School

One of the important recommendations of the Commission has been to establish Multipurpose Higher Secondary Schools for varied and diversified interests of students. Preferably each district should have one such school. In rural areas, schools should have agriculture as an important subject. Home science should be made compulsory for girls.

Curriculum

The Commission recommended for the reorganisation of the curriculum taking into view the interests of the students, the demands of the times and the community.

The Commission suggested Maths, General Science, Languages, Social Studies, Physical Education, Crafts, etc. at the lower secondary level and diversified groups of subjects at the higher secondary level which would be as follows:

- Humanities
- Sciences
- Industrial subjects
- Commerce
- Agriculture
- Fine Arts
- Home Science.

Textbooks

The Commission has recommended for the constitution of a high powered committee for selecting textbooks for secondary schools. The committee will consist of—a High Court judge, a member of the Public Service Commission, a Vice-Chancellor, a principal of a government institution, two educationist and the Director of public instruction of schools. The Commission laid down the basis of selection such as production, printing, paper used, illustrations and pictures and above all, the content. The textbooks according to the Commission should not be changed soon.

Administration and Finance

The Commission made elaborate recommendations on school administration and finance. It stressed the need for effective and qualitative inspection and instead of finding fault, it should guide the teachers. On finance, it suggested that the Central Government should give aid to the States.

Teachers

The Commission also emphasized the need to improve the socio-economic status of the teachers by giving them good pay. Other service benefits should be given to teachers. The teachers' retirement age should be 60 years. It also recommended for improvement in their training. The number of teaching days should not be less than 200 in a year.

The Commission made valuable suggestions to improve secondary education, though the problems in secondary education could not be removed in toto. But this is a good effort in the direction.

National Education Commission, 1964-66

India ushered in the era of planned development. With this aim, five-year plans were launched. The execution of plans brought to our knowledge the inherent weaknesses in education. The government of India appointed an Education Commission in 1964 under the chairmanship of Dr. D.S. Kothari. The Commission is also known as "Education Commission". It was appointed on July 14, 1964. The Commission had eminent educationists, experts and social activists. J.P. Naik was the member secretary. The Commission undertook a study of several aspects of education. The report is divided into three parts. The first part has six chapters and deals with reorganisation of education and other issues. The second part has eleven chapters and deals with different stages and areas of education. The third part deals with suggestions. From this it is clear that the report is very comprehensive and touches nearly all aspects of education.

Education and National Aims

On education and national aims, the Commission asserted that education can help in solving the problems of our country. The Commission recommended the following programmes to achieve national aims. The national aims are as follows:

- Self-sufficiency in food products.
- Economic development and end of unemployment.
- Social and Political unity.
- Political development.

To achieve these national aims, a programme of action has been suggested.

The programme of Action are as follows :

- Increase in production through education.
- Social and political integration through education.
- Strengthening democracy through education.
- Acceleration of the pace of modernization through education.
- Development of social, moral and spiritual values through education.

Educational Structure

On educational structure and raising of standards at different levels, the Commission gave several suggestions but its two suggestions on secondary education deserve special attention.

- Provision of national education at the secondary stage.
- There should be only one public examination. On higher education, it suggested that it should begin after 12 years, i.e. general education for 10 years and 2 years of higher secondary education. It also recommended for the provision of better facilities of education to students.

Teacher Status

The Commission regretted the condition and the status of teachers in the society and suggested for their improvement as follows:

- The Government should fix minimum pay for a teacher.
- The Centre should help the States financially so that they are at par with the Central Government teachers.
- There should be principle of equality in pay for the teachers.
- To draw good and qualified people to the profession, they should be given the same pay which people of the same qualifications get in other services of the Government.

The Commission also gave suggestions for raising their status, their chances of promotions, retirement benefits and improvement in the working conditions. The beginning, according to the commission, is to be made from primary school teachers who are badly affected.

Teacher Education

While stressing the importance of teacher education, the Commission has pointed out the defects of vocational education. According to the Commission, training institutions are in bad shape, they lacks able teachers, curriculum is lifeless and uninteresting, too much theorization and lack of practical experiments. The defects can be removed only through the end of isolation of teacher education, improvement in training programme, fixation of duration of training for different category of teachers and improvement in the conditions of training institutions.

Enrolment and Manpower

According to the Commission, "One of the important programmes in national reconstruction is the development of human resources". For this, education cannot have limits. In India the Commission noted the increase in student population which requires a national enrolment policy which should ensure seven years free and compulsory education to every child. The Commission also suggested enrolment policies at different stages of education.

Equalisation of Educational Opportunities

In every democratic and civilized society every individual needs to be treated equally. The Commission has rightly recommended that constitutional provision of free and compulsory education to children of the school going age should be pursued. It recommended for the provision of free supply of books to poor children, scholarships and stipends to bright students. These steps according to the Commission would help the deprived class to make progress. It also recommended for help to the physically handicapped children.

Curriculum

The Commission stressed the need for reorganisation of curriculum at all stages of education. These stages are as follows:

Lower Primary Stage

Language (Mother tongue or regional language or provincial language), simple mathematics, study of environment, creative activities, work experience and health education.

Higher Primary Stage

Languages (Mother tongue and Hindi or English) Maths, Sciences, Social Studies, Craft work and social services, physical education, education in moral and spiritual values.

Lower Secondary Stage

Three languages, Maths, Sciences, History, Civics, Geography, Craft work experience, Physical education and Moral education.

Higher Secondary Stage

Languages, any three subjects from any diversified group, work experience, physical education, Craft and moral education.

The Commission has recommended a three language formula, i.e. Mother tongue or regional language, official language of the union, a modern Indian or European language.

Teaching Methods

With regard to improvement in teaching methods, the Commission recommended to make it flexible and dynamic. This is possible only when the teacher comes forward. Innovation and research should be encouraged. The Commission regretted the shortage of good textbooks particularly in sciences. A normal programme for preparing textbooks should be taken up on the lines of NCERT. Suitable remuneration should be paid for writing books. It also recommended sale of textbooks through school co-operatives. Radio broadcasts should be arranged for teachers and pupils. The Commission accepted guidance and counselling as one of the essential elements of education. Its aim should be to help students on different occasions. Guidance bureau should be set up under competent people.

Evaluation

The Commission considered evaluation as an important aspect of education but it requires improvement. The present system is full of defects. The Commission recommended the use of such techniques through which the students performances can be evaluated which otherwise cannot be evaluated in the prevailing system. At the higher secondary level, verbal and diagnostic tests should be held. The Commission suggested that report cards should be maintained.

School Administration and Supervision

The Commission has recommended a four point programme for effective administration and supervision. They are:

- Common school system of public education.
- A nation wide programme for school improvement.
- Supervision.
- Separation of inspection from administration.

Higher Education: Objective and Improvement

The Commission has recommended on different aspects of higher education such as objectives of universities, development of major universities, improvement of other universities and affiliated colleges, improvement of teaching and evaluation, medium of instruction, student services, students' union, students' discipline, etc. The Commission's recommendations on the above are valuable.

The Commission has also recommended the introduction of part-time education through correspondence or through evening classes. Post-graduate education and research should be taken up only by such universities, which can provide it effectively. The Commission recommended for rapid expansion of women education, they should be given stipend and scholarships as well. Courses should be of their choice.

The Commission recommended for the establishment of more universities in order to reduce over crowding. It also recommended for the provision of educational research. Incentives should be given for this. The Commission was of the view that the universities should enjoy autonomy so that they may pursue academic activities properly. With regard to finance, the Commission recommended that the State Government should provide sufficient funds in this regard so that it can help the universities. The Commission also opined about the appointment of vice-chancellors, functioning of affiliated colleges, different kinds of colleges, Inter-university, Board, UGC, etc.

Education for Agriculture

The Commission recommended for an action plan for education for agriculture. It recommended for the establishment of rural universities in each State, establishment of agriculture colleges and agriculture Polytechnics, provision for education of agriculture in primary and secondary schools. It also recommended to take up extension programmes in order to provide information on agriculture.

Other subjects which were also studied by the Commission are technical, Engineering and vocational education, science education and research and adult-education. The Commission made recommendations on educational administration and finance. The Commission emphasised the need of educational planning in a country like India. A national policy should be evolved. Role of private enterprises in education should be encouraged, as their contribution is immense.

The Commission also discussed the role of Central Government in education, as education is a State subject. It should work for the growth of scientific, technological and vocational education in the country. It should also plan the development of agriculture and made some recommendations for the effective and co-ordinated working. On finance, the Commission recommended four and half times increase in educational expenditures to meet the growing requirements of education, it also recommended to generate income for education through other sources as well. The Commission urged for allocation of funds on certain principles and misuse and that wastage of funds should be checked.

The Commission's recommendations as discussed above in short are very important. Justice M.Chagla, the former Minister of Education, Union Government described it's as "The Magna Charta" of education for teachers, for it made several suggestions for improvement in their status. It also laid great stress on the development of modern sciences, which is the need of the present times. But it is deplorable that the Commission did not accept basic education. Most of the members of the Commission were from foreign countries who didn't understand the cultural ethos of the country and that is why some of its recommendations were found to be very ambitious.

National Policy on Education (1986) and its Revised Form (1992)

There was a rapid expansion of education and also the country was rocked by the explosion of population. Rise in educated and uneducated, unemployment was shattering the tranquil waters of the country. Education was not helping in the removal of defects. Besides it was lagging behind in many aspects from the changes going on in the world educational scene. The world was in the grip of technological scientific and computer revolution. At this time the country had a very young, dynamic, charismatic and forward looking leader, Shri Rajiv Gandhi as the Prime Minister of India. He wanted to take India to great heights of scientific and technological progress.

The Parliament of India during the budget session in 1986 discussed and adopted the National Policy on Education, 1986. The document consists of 12 parts and deals at length with several aspects of education. In many respects, it is innovative and path breaking. It has recommended some radical changes in the system. In the beginning the NPE lays down the essence and role of education as following:

- "Education for All" is our national perspective. It is fundamental to material and spiritual development.
- Education has an acculturating role, refines sensitivities and perceptions.
- Education develops manpower for different levels of the economy.

- Education is a unique investment in the present and the future which is the key to NPE.

National System of Education

Under this system, all students irrespective of caste, creed, sex and location have to be ensured education upto a given level. It envisages a common structure of education in the country of 10+2+3 (Five years elementary education, five years lower secondary, two years higher secondary and three years degree course). NSE will be based on a national curricular framework with a common core along with other components. Secular values will be given weightage. Equality of opportunities will be provided to all without any discrimination. Minimum level of learning (MLL) will be laid down for each stage of education. Inter regional mobility will be facilitated in higher education in general and technical education in particular. In the field of research and development and education in science and technology special measures will be taken. Universalization of elementary education, adult literacy, education to housewives, agricultural and industrial workers will be taken up. Distance education would be encouraged. Key educational institutions will be strengthened. A better co-ordination between States and the Centre will be ensured.

The NPE has also made elaborate plans for women's education by removing disparities, the education of scheduled castes and scheduled tribes, minorities and other educationally backward sections and the handicapped.

Adult Education

The NPE has stressed the need and importance of adult education to remove adult illiteracy among Indian masses. The NPE proposes to launch mass literacy campaign with the cooperation and involvement of the whole society. A vast programme for the establishment of adult education centres in rural area will be launched. The use of Radio, T.V. and films, creation of learners' groups, programmes of distance learning, etc. will be promoted.

Reorganisation of Child Education and Elementary Education

NPE gives importance to Early Child Care Programme of Early Child Care and Education (ECCE) which will be taken up. This will be child oriented, focused on maintaining the individuality of the child. Elementary education will get a new thrust. It will emphasize on two aspects:

- Universal enrolment and universal education of children upto 14 years of age.
- A substantial improvement in the quality of education. The approach will be child-oriented. In order to strengthen and make elementary education more attractive, purposeful and rewarding, some essential facilities like two large classrooms, toys, black-boards, maps, charts, learning materials, etc. will be provided along with two teachers, one of them to be woman.

Non-formal Education

A large and systematic programme of NFE will be launched for school dropouts, working children and girls. This will be strengthened through various efforts.

Secondary Education

Realising the importance of secondary education the NPE proposes to formulate curricula to bring about work culture to vocationalise education, to provide valuable manpower for economic growth.

Vocationalisation

The NPE feels that the introduction of systematic, well planned and vigorously implemented programmes of vocational education is crucial in the proposed educational reorganisation. According to it, the vocational education will be a distinct stream intended to prepare for occupations, spanning several areas of activities. The responsibility will be of the government as well as of employers. Graduates of vocational courses will be given opportunities for professional growth and career improvement.

Higher Education

In the context of the unprecedented explosion of knowledge, the NPE recommends it to become dynamic as never before, constantly entering uncharted areas. Looking to the vast number of colleges and universities in India it proposed to expand facilities in the existing institutions. Autonomy to be introduced in the departments of the colleges affiliated to the universities, courses will be redesigned to meet the demands of specialisation better. Seats in these institutions will be filled strictly on the basis of merit. Research in different fields will be given enhanced support.

Open Universities and Distance Learning

Educational opportunities will be made available to large number of people through Open University and distance learning centres. Indira Gandhi National Open University will be strengthened.

Delinking Degrees from Jobs

This is a landmark suggestion in the National Policy on Education. Delinking will be applied in services in which a university degree need not be a necessary qualification.

Reorienting the Content and Process of Education

The NPE opines that the pre-occupation with modern technologies cannot be allowed to serve our new generation from the roots in Indian history and culture. Therefore, the curriculum and process of education will be enriched by cultural content. Children will be enabled to develop sensitivity to beauty, harmony and refinement.

Value Education

Expressing its concern over the erosion of essential values and increasing cynicism to society, the NPE focuses on the need to re-adjustment in the curriculum for the cultivation of social and moral values.

The NPE has also given due importance to work experience, awareness of environmental problems, mathematics teaching, science and physical education. It has stressed the need to strengthen these.

Examination Reform

The objective should be to recast the examination system so as to ensure a method of assessment, a method to eliminate excessive element of chance and subjectivity, to de-emphasis memorisation. Continuous and comprehensive evaluation for scholastic and non-scholastic aspects of education should be introduced along with semester system.

The Teacher

The NPE proposed to enhance the status of the working conditions of teachers and training of the teachers. It recommends a plan of continuous teacher education. It also proposes the establishment of District Institute of Education (DIET) for training of teachers. In the end the NPE also deals with management of education at different levels.

TOTAL IMPACT ON EDUCATION

After the adoption of the National Policy on Education, 1986, the Ministry of Human Resource Development came forward with a programme of action on the NPE in the Monsoon Session of the Parliament. Programme of action document details the resolve for the implementation of the NPE in the country. Some of the important developments after the implementation are detailed below briefly:

Primary Education

Under the universalisation of elementary education (UEE), an ambitious programme "Operation Black Board" has been launched in the country to strengthen primary education. Basically OBB is a very innovative programme through which essential facilities are provided at the primary stage. These included construction, addition, alteration, of the school buildings in the rural areas. Provision of two teachers, one male and the other female to each school has been made. Several teaching, sports, recreational, materials have also been provided.

Secondary Education

- Navodaya Vidyalayas have been established in rural areas on the pattern of public schools for the better education of rural students.

- Vocationalisation of secondary education: Vocational courses have been introduced at +2 stages in higher secondary schools in the country. These schools have separate staff. Provisions for workshop for each trade have been made. Other inputs such as libraries, practical experiences, linkages with industries, etc. have been made.

Higher Education

Institutions are being strengthened, autonomous colleges have been named, open universities are established, facilities for distance education have been strengthened. Indira Gandhi National Open University (IGNOU) in New Delhi, Kota Open University (KOU) in Rajasthan and Bhoj Open University (BOU) in Madhya Pradesh are examples.

Training

At the school education level, training colleges are being strengthened, contents of training are reorganised. The most important changes in training programmes for the lower secondary and primary school teachers is the establishment of DIETs in each district which provide continuous training to teachers in pre-service and in-service. Orientation programmes for teachers on massive scale have been organised.

Literary Programmes

Eradication of illiteracy has received priority in the post-NPE era. Non-formal education, adult education centres, and other welfare programmes aim to literate the masses.

In short, the NPE has been very vigorously implemented in the country and a great progress has been noticed in areas such as mass literacy, early child care education, UEE, NFE awareness of environmental health, women education, technical education, vocationalisation, etc.

EDUCATION IN THE EMERGING INDIA

Today India is emerging as a super power in the field of information technology. It is also rated as a nuclear giant in the world. It has advanced in the space technology and only comparable to a few countries. Industrially also the country has made astonishing progress. Indian students, technicians, engineers, medicos, etc. are very bright and some have proved to be geniuses in their fields. Despite all this, there are contradictions and disparities in several sectors of Indian society. Many of the past efforts to iron them out have not been very rewarding. What should be education in the new emerging India is undoubtedly very difficult to say. However, some picture of a distant future can be easily visualised.

Population Education

Since the last century, the population in this sub-continent in general and particularly in India had been constantly rising. Before partition the undivided India had a population of 36 crores and the remaining India was nearly 26 crore. It started quantum jumps from 1951 when it was 51 crores. After 50 years the population of India has crossed the figure of one billion. The situation is very much alarming. Many reasons, such as better health conditions, improvement in nutrition, eradication of epidemics, growth in life expectancy, etc. may be assigned for the steep rise in population, but its explosion is threatening development and environment which make up an important element in the construction of a new social and economic order today.

During the past six decades though India has tried to checkmate the growth at times forcibly and also most of the times through awareness programmes, results have not been satisfactory. Education plays an important role in awakening the consciousness in developing the right kind of responses and initiatives. So far population education has been including understanding of reproduction, child nursing, health problems, advantages of small family, awareness of family planning programmes, etc. Now it is time that new thrust be given to population education. Population education should be extended to every home in the country, every village should be educated and covered. A massive programme that too a time bound programme should be undertaken. The present curriculum, methods of routine and dull teaching should be reorganised.

Environment Education

It is a paradox that a country like India which was rich in environment, is today facing the agony of pollution of environment. The posterity will make researches to find out the places of mountains, rivers and varieties of trees. We have reached this sorry state due to mad drive of urbanisation and industrialisation. Industries are necessary to our economy and prosperity but it suffocates human beings, the end of human species is clearly in sight.

The emerging picture of India in the coming decades is of multi-storied concrete jungles of huge structures and mansions where air for breathing would be scarce and probably sold. We must understand that environmental problem is not limited to a city or a state or even a country, it is a global problem, it is a problem of the entire humanity. Since 1915 efforts for formulating human ecology are going on but today the entire global society is beset with this problem.

Environmental education in India is not a new concept. Even in the ancient system of education, great emphasis was laid on the enrichment and protection of environment. The main objective of environmental education today should be to understand the relationship between man and nature. Ex-President of USA Nixon once called for the development of environmental literacy. He said, "environmental education is the process of recognising values and clarifying concepts in order to develop skills and attitudes necessary to understand and appreciate the inter-relations among man, his culture and his bio-physical surroundings".

Curriculum on environmental education should be reorganised to include resource management, ecological and environmental problems due to urbanisation, industrialisation, deforestation and intensive agriculture, and their remedies. Also courses in ecology, conservation, soil sciences should be introduced at all levels of education to bring about mass awareness. Methods of teaching cannot be prescribed but it should stress more on experiences and should be activity based. Students should learn through experiences of air pollution, water pollution, soil pollution, sound pollution, mental pollution and environmental pollution through industries.

Education and Modernisation

India today is on the cross-roads of modernisation. Our space crafts are revolving round the universe, but our masses are illiterate and ignorant of these scientific and technological developments.

Modernity cannot be grafted on ignorance and illiteracy and the promise of building a just and egalitarian society will be meaningless till the basic equality of educational opportunity is provided to every one irrespective of class, caste, sex and race. The Constitution of India had promised the fulfillment of this dream within ten years of its commencement but even after the end of the last century, we are not even near the 50% of the target. The new century has begun and the goal is still not in sight. Though the per capita income has increased and the number of people below the poverty line has somewhat decreased, a large number of people are still ill-clad, ill-fed and live a shelterless life, oblivious of the progress in different fields. In this background, the country's march towards modernisation vis-à-vis the role of education has to be understood.

People are not unanimous about the concept of modernisation. Economists view it as man's application of new technologies to acquire dominance over nature and to bring about a marked increase in the gross national product per capita. According to political scientists, the ways used by the Governments to increase their capacity to innovate and adapt to change led to modernisation as "the process by which historically evolved institutions are adapted to the rapidly changing functions that reflect the unprecedented increase in man's knowledge permitting control over his environment that accompanied the scientific revolution". In some, modernisation is a revolutionary process, it is essentially a process, a movement from the traditional, quasi-traditional order to certain desired types of technology and associated forms of social structure, value orientation, motivations and norms. In India, modernisation has led to the change of lifestyles, thinking processes, a break from traditions and cultural norms.

Education has a vital role to play. Education must lay emphasis on the compromise between the past and the present and also endeavour to a harmonious future. Kothari Commission said, "Human being is dynamic and progressing. Society is also an ever-changing phenomenon. It cannot remain static and stereotype. The structure is subject incessant change, growing delay, finding renewal, accommodating itself to the...modification in the course of time". Hence, education must be reoriented to meet the challenges of social changes and to help in building a social order based on equality, liberty and justice.

Education has also to take stock of the menace of growing polarisation of the caste system. The political parties are playing them up for narrow political ends. Indeed a large section of the people had been neglected and ignored but exploitation is not the solution. It may lead to social, and communal discord and disharmony. Education, which is an effective tool of modernisation has to expand and cover every section of the society. It is only through education that the views and behavioural changes of all sections of people can help in building an egalitarian society, free from mutual distrust, hatred and animosity. Women neglected and ignored have also to be brought, to the mainstream.

The emergence of working women and their socio-economic role in the family so far did not attract any attention but in the emerging Indian society maintenance of family ties, harmony in the family and the society will have to form an important agenda of education. The emancipation of women, the demand of women to have greater representation in the legislative bodies and governance of India require a fresh look. Education must be vibrant, dynamic, flexible to meet any challenges of the future.

Trends and Process of Education in Indian Society

4

Man, a social and thinking being, is a product of evolution of Nature. Starting his career as a creature of the environment around three million years ago, he has become its moulder. At no time has the human society remained stagnant or static but it has been ever dynamic to meet the challenges of changing times and new needs so that the society continues to survive and progress. Being the thinker of Nature, it has become conscious of not only of his own unfolding but of the entire Nature and its existence and the future possibilities.

Meaning of Society

Society is a term used commonly by people. But when we ask what does society mean, then many will not be able to answer. Different people may give answers, which may vary from one another. Let us, find out what does society mean?

We might have defined society as one of the following or something similar:

- a group of people living in a definite territory,
- an organised group of individuals residing together in a territory,
- an organised group of individuals can be called a society only when its members live together for a long periods,
- an organised group of individuals residing together in a territory not only for long periods but also have common interests, share common historical and cultural heritage, and observe common tradition and customs,
- a group of people living in a definite territory, having a common culture, customs and language,

- an organised group of people having some kind of commonality in the basic conditions of life of individual members—their dress, the method of living, thinking, behaving and interacting,
- a system whereby people live together in organised community,
- particular grouping of humanity following same customs, laws and ethics,
- a community having common traditions, institutions and interests.

We attempt to define a society in the right direction. A society means all these and many more.

It is obvious that a society is not simply a collective term for a number of individuals at a place. Can passengers travelling in a train or soldiers living in an Army Camp constitute a society? We need systematic study to understand the true meaning of society. *Sociology is concerned with the scientific study of the nature and development of society and social behaviour.*

Definitions of Society

- **Laski.** A group of human beings living together for the satisfaction of their mutual wants.
- **Leacock.** Not only political relations by which men are bound together but the whole range of human relations and collective activities.
- **G.D.H. Cole.** The complex organised association and institutions within the community.
- **S.F. Nidel.** By society we can only mean an aggregate of human beings bound together in some unity, that is, acting in an integrated and regular manner and possessed of some degree of permanence and stability.
- **Sri Aurobindo.** A society, a great human collectivity is an organic being with a common soul, mind and body.

Society and Sociology

Society is a great human collectivity having a common culture, customs and a medium of communication. Its continuity and increase in time are ensured through the marriage process and procedure accepted by the society. It is an organised interdependent unit of people having common interests, sharing common historical and cultural heritage, observing common tradition and custom and living by its own norms and modes necessary for the welfare and progress of people. These common tendencies provide unity and coherence in the society and generate common aspirations. There is a continuous interaction between the members of society as they communicate with one another and discuss common social events and issues. It leads to the phenomenon of social life. The nature of social life depends upon the nature of interaction the members of society indulge in. Open social life of the open societies depend upon the free and frank interactions among members and vice-versa. Hence, a society has the following main features:

- Common Territory.
- Common Historical and Cultural Heritage.
- Communication Skill, Language.
- Close Interaction.
- Common Customs.
- Unity and Affinity.
- Code of Social Behaviour and Social Life.
- Common Aspiration.

Sociology is an academic discipline concerned with the systematic study of man and society. It attempts to understand and determine the course of civilization and culture. Physical Anthropologists, Socio-biologists, Ethnologists, Culture Historians, Linguists, Human Ecologists, other Social Scientists, Social Psychologists try to study and attempt to unravel the missing links and throw light on different aspects of human society and evolve a clear picture. The core field of sociology is 'Social Organisation'. It includes the entire range of human groups from the smallest family to the more complex nation state including religious, educational, industrial, and political institutions as well as the larger global unit of mankind.

Society and State

Society precedes the state as it precedes the church, the corporation, the political party. What is the relation between the society and the state? What is the difference between the two? See Table 4.1.

Table 4.1: Relationship Between Society and State

Society	*State*
• Social organisation.	• Political organisation.
• Concerned with social order.	• Concerned with political order.
• Prior to state.	• Emerges from the society.
• Does not possess sovereignty.	• Possesses sovereignty.
• Wider than the state.	• Narrower than the society.
• Territory is not essential.	• Territory is the essential basis.
• May be organised or unorganised.	• Organisation is essential for the state.

Social Stratification

Social stratification is a characteristic feature of human society. It is characterised by the following:

- it is not simply a function of individual differences,
- it persists over generations, stems from society,
- it is universal but not uniform,
- it involves not just inequality but also beliefs.

The Davis-Moore Thesis

The Davis-Moore Thesis asserts that social stratification is universal because it has beneficial consequences for the operation of a society. Otherwise, how can one explain the fact that some form of social stratification is found everywhere. Various categories of occupations exist in a society. The greater the functional importance of occupation, the more rewards a society attaches to it. This is the basis of unequal distribution of resources in a society. Rewarding important work with income, prestige, power, leisure encourages people to do them. The resulting unequal distribution of resources in a society motivates people to the most significant work and they strive to work better and harder. This system of unequal distribution of resources due to variation in the quality of work is, in fact, amounts to social stratification. Such a society with the system of unequal rewards is a most productive one.

Different Social Systems

Social stratification is characterised by *caste systems* and *class systems*. There are no pure caste or class systems. Elements of both can be seen in UK.

The Caste System in India

The Society is organised into castes. Caste system is, in general, the characteristic feature of agrarian societies. People are born into one of several thousand caste groups. The shape of peoples' life are greatly influenced and determined by the castes to which they are born:

- Families belonging to a caste generally perform work handed over from generation to generation. In an agrarian society, generally, some vocation like farming may be open to everyone. But generally the castes are recognised by the type of work their members do (Barber, ironsmith, goldsmith, carpenter, leather worker, potter, washer-man, priests, etc.).
- People marry within the same caste (endogamous).
- People generally believe that their life's desires and aspirations will be fulfilled through performing their duties sincerely which have been provided to them automatically.
- People feel pride in their caste and trace their ancestry to a saint or rishi born in the past and try to emulate the values for which he attained fame.
- People believe that their birth into a caste is no bar to rise to any height in the realisation of four purusharthas: *dharma*, *artha*, *kama* and *moksha*.

Transportation and mobility, newer economical opportunities, opening of facilities to acquire new skills have loosened the hold of traditional work in rural society in India and people are migrating to urban areas in search of new pastures. Caste system, so far as jobs and social position are concerned, has lost their meaning.

Class System in UK

England, during the Middle Ages, was characterised by a cast like system of three estates:

First estate or a hereditary nobility: There were 150 families of nobles constituting only 5 per cent of population but controlling most of the land. It was the chief form of wealth.

Second estate or clergy: The clergy was endowed with the church's extensive landholding in addition to his spiritual power.

Third estate or commoners: Most commoners were serfs who worked on plots of land owned by the nobles. They remained mostly illiterates having little access to schooling.

The Industrial Revolution brought about a sea change. The economy boomed. Some commoners living in cities earned enough wealth to rival the nobility. Money, schooling and legal rights brought about a change in the traditional social ranking to class system. But the legacy of feudal past remains in the present social hierarchy.

Apartheid in South Africa

The society in South Africa in recent past was dominated by apartheid which is based on racial differences. It is now in the decline. Racial differences appears now and then in many countries in the world.

Classless Society: The Experiment that Failed (Former USSR)

Former Soviet Union (USSR) claimed to have formed a classless society with the abolishing of social hierarchy by transforming private farm, factories and other productive property to public (state) property during *Communist Rule* from 1917 to 1994. There was no social inequality. But the former USSR had a different kind of social hierarchy:

- high government official at the top,
- intellectuals and professionals,

- manual workers, and
- rural peasants.

The above categories had different living standards.

SOCIETY IN TIME

From the Age of Food Gathering Stage to the Age of Cybernetics

Early man was a 'Creature' of the environment. The erect posture of man liberated his forelimbs from locomotor functions and through his opposable thumbs he could manipulate tools which served as detachable hands without affecting his body. It led to the development of his brain. Besides perceptual thought, he developed conceptual thinking power. Empowered with the enormous power of manipulative skills and mental faculties man dominated the scene and starting his career as a *creature of the environment turned into its moulder* and built his own environment—the psychosocial, social, socio-cultural or man-made or built environment. It includes everything developed by man through the application of his thinking faculties and tools—family, social, religious, economic, educational and political organisations; language and technology, the conscious, sub-conscious and super-conscious organisations of mind; as well as ideas, knowledge, will, cultures and civilizations, along with physical infrastructure. Three million years of man's existence on earth has passed through five successive stages of development through five main technological innovations:

- Hunting and Gathering.
- Horticulture and Pastoralism.
- Agriculture.
- Industry.
- Information Technology (Cybernetics).

Three million years of human existence is a story of the ever increasing energy and material needs of man to meet his increasing material wants and hunger for affluence.

Age of Food Gathering Stage

The primitive, oldest and productive technology in human society was *Hunting and Gathering* when man used simple tools for hunting animals and gathering vegetation. This stage is still prevalent in several extant societies in many countries including India. For the primitive man muscular energy was the only source of energy. It was replenished regularly through his intake of food. This conversion of food into muscular energy was confined to the natural process of energy flow in the bio-sphere as man was still a creature of the environment and a link in the food chain and food web of the living world. Hunting, fishing and collecting edible fruits, flowers, leaves, roots and tubers formed their chief sources of food. For these purposes they used tools which they made from available hard-rock pieces, poles and hard skeletal materials. They belonged to food gathering stage. In addition to food, the hunting man needed energy to roast his prey and also for warmth. This he procured through converting wood into fire.

Age of Horticulture and Pastoralism

The Age of Horticulture and Pastoralism emerged when man learnt the technology to raise crops using hand tools (Horticulture) and the technology to domesticate animals (Pastoralism). It took more than a million years for the primitive food-gathering man to domesticate plants and animals. Hardly twenty to fifteen thousand years ago the technology of Horticulture and Pastoralism might have started evolving.

The chance discovery of sprouting from the seeds thrown near habitation after eating fruits might have led to the planting of fruit trees. In course of time, it would have led to the development of horticulture with the invention of hoe and digging stick especially in the fertile regions of the globe. In arid regions hunting might have led to domestication of animals. Many societies in Asia, Africa and America blended both horticulture and domestication.

Greater productivity from horticulture and domestication of animals allowed human society to expand its numbers to hundreds. Though pastoral societies moved from one place to another, i.e., they led nomadic life, the horticulturists were rooted to the crop field, and made permanent settlement. Hierarchy developed in these societies with concentration of wealth in a few families. Surplus food production freed many people to engage in crafts, trade and priesthood as whole-time jobs.

Age of Agriculture

From horticultural and pastoral man to agricultural man is a logical step. Agriculture emerged with the invention of plow. Plows harnessed to animals turn the soil and keep the land to be farmed fertile and for many years crops are grown which provide food to thousands of people. It led human societies to live in permanent settlements in large numbers. Agricultural man entered into newer pathways of energy flow in nature. In addition to food and fire for cooking, the agricultural man turned grass into the muscular energy of draft animals to till his fields and transportation of materials. Agriculture and domestication of animals progressed side by side. As he progressed further, he utilised wind and water to move wind-mills, sails and water-mills.

Large amount of surplus food production and transportation could support large number of non-agricultural people which led to the development of urban concentrations. With agriculture, emerged human civilisations. The discovery of a submerged ancient city dated 7500 BC off the Gujarat Coast in the Gulf of Cambay probably makes India the fount of human civilisation. The contemporaries of the Cambay society were hunters learning the art of cultivation.

Age of Industrial Revolution

The advent of the steam engine heralded the Industrial Revolution. The enormous amount of energy needed by industrial man for rapid industrial growth were obtained by the exploitation of the fossil fuels—coal, petroleum and natural gas. Not only fossil fuels but also other energy sources, especially hydro and nuclear energy were used to generate electricity. Solar energy by direct conversion, tidal energy and geothermal energy from volcanoes and hot springs also utilized lately. In agrarian societies manipulation of land was the principal economic activity, but in industrial societies manipulation and maintenance of machine became principal economic activity. Educational opportunities increased and became accessible to many.

Age of Cybernetics

The advent of high speed electronic computer ushered the age of IT Revolution (Cybernetics). It is hardly ten to fifteen thousand years ago that agriculture might have been invented. The IT Revolution evolved during the last 3 to 4 decades. It has given rise to the quaternary sector of economy bringing about a shift of principal economic activities from manipulation of land to manipulation of machine to manipulation of information. Society of human beings has been gradually evolving from primitive food gathering stage to the present cybernetics stage due to the development of Science and Technology, means of communication and transport and due to the advanced organisational skills gained from training and education. But modern technology is threatening labour.

Primitive Society

In the primitive society man utilised the caves and trees in the jungles for his shelter to live and protect himself and his family from animals around. He had to hunt for food every day like other animals for his survival. The main characteristics of primitive society man were as follows:

- He lived in natural and rustic setting, in caves and trees in jungles, along with his family.
- He had limited skills of survival based on his experience; he had acquired skills to make tiny tools from rock pieces for hunting and other needs.
- He always lived in fear of animals and natural calamities.
- He had no organised social and economic institutions.
- He had limited language and communication skills.
- He had less developed faculties of mind.

Modern Society

The modern society is endowed with new knowledge of science and new inventions of technology. There is total change in modern human life due to growth of urbanization, industrialization, mobilization, quicker transportation, instant communication, organization of Government wedded to welfare of citizens, international co-operation and globalisation. The man of modern society today enjoys all the amenities of life such as comfortable housing, electricity, transport and telecommunications. He has access to the following privileges of modern age:

- He has comfortable living in the urban setting.
- He has developed better intelligence and skills through training and education.
- He has acquired rights of protection and property to live a secure and comfortable life.
- He enjoys benefit of many well organised institutions like family, school, church, Government, bank, etc.
- He has better environment and more resources to enjoy higher standards of living.
- He has more mobility in social and economic aspects of life.
- He has access to the use of many sophisticated tools and machines like computers in various fields of activities.

In modern era modern man had the advantage of long experience of evolution and scientific knowledge available in modern age. Industrial Revolution brought industrialisation and modernisation of human society. Man has now entered into the age of Computer and Information Technology Revolution.

Characteristics of the Modern Civilised and Cultured Man

The characteristics of the modern civilised man are as follows. He is able to:

- Develop scientific knowledge and acquire skills to solve many problems of life.
- Use technology available for comfortable life and efficient performance in every field of life.
- Organise himself fairly well politically, socially and economically.
- Develop skills of sharing and caring for his family members and fellow beings in his community.

- Develop a good sense of social responsibility and sensitivity to problems of community.
- Improve his surroundings and working conditions through the professional groups and unions in every field.
- Take advantage of higher learning in every field to ensure better quality of life from time to time and realise his mission and aspiration.

The Cycle of Society

The evolution of human society is guided by the inherent evolutionary forces of mental evolution. On the basis of European and particularly German history the theorist Lamprecht supposed that human society progresses through certain distinct psychological stages. He termed these stages as:

- Symbolic
- Typal
- Conventional
- Individualist
- Subjective.

Analysing its validity, Sri Aurobindo in his treaties, *The Human Cycle*, argues, "This development forms, then, a sort of psychological cycle through which a nation or a civilisation is bound to proceed. Obviously, such classifications likely to err by rigidity and to substitute a material straight line for the coils and zigzags of Nature. The psychology of man and his societies is too complex, too synthetical of many-sided and intermixed tendencies to satisfy any such rigorous and formal analysis. Nor does this theory of a psychological cycle tell us what is the inner meaning of its successive phases or the necessity of their succession or the term and end towards which they are driving. But still to understand natural laws whether of Mind or Matter it is necessary to analyse their working into its discoverable elements, main constituents, dominant forces, though these may not actually be found anywhere in isolation. I will leave aside the western thinker's own dealings with his idea. The suggestive names he has offered us, if we examine their intrinsic sense and value, may yet throw some light on the thickly veiled secret of our historic evolution, and this is the line on which it would be most useful to investigate".

Undoubtedly, wherever we can seize human society in what seems to us its primitive beginnings or early stages, no matter whether the race is comparatively cultured or savage or economically advanced or backward, we do find a strongly symbolic mentality that governs or at least pervades its thought, customs and institutions. Symbolic, but of what? We find that this social stage is always religious and actively imaginative in its religion; for symbolism and a widespread imaginative or intuitive religious feeling have a natural kinship and especially in earlier or primitive formations they have always gone together. When man begins to be predominantly intellectual, sceptical, ratiocinative, he is already preparing for an individualist society and the age of symbols and the age of conventions have passed or are losing their virtue.

The symbol then is of something which man feels to be present behind himself and his life and his activities- the Divine, the God, the vast and deep unamenable, a hidden, living and mysterious nature of things. All his religious and social institutions, all the moments and phases of his life are to him symbols in which he seeks to express what he knows or guesses of the mystic influences that are behind his life and shape and govern or at the least intervene in its movements.

"From this symbolic attitude came the tendency to make everything in society a sacrament, religious and sacrosanct, but as yet with a large and vigorous freedom in all its forms,—a freedom which we do not find in the rigidity of "savage" communities because these have already passed out of the symbolic into the conventional stage though on a curve of degeneration instead of a curve of growth. The spiritual idea govern all; the symbolic religious forms which support it are fixed in principle; the social forms are lax, free and capable of infinite development. One thing, however, begins to progress towards a firm fixity and this is the psychological type. Thus, we have first the symbolic idea of the four orders, expressing—to employ an abstractly figurative language which the Vedic thinkers would not have used nor perhaps understood, but which helps best our modern understanding—the Divine as knowledge in man, the Divine as power, the Divine as production, enjoyment and mutuality, the Divine as service, obedience and work.

These divisions answer to four cosmic principles, the Wisdom that conceives the order and principle of things, the Power that sanctions, upholds and enforces it, the Harmony that creates the arrangement of its parts, the Work that carries out what the rest direct. Next, out of this idea there developed a firm but not yet rigid social order based primarily upon temperament and psychic type *guna* with a corresponding ethical discipline and secondarily upon the social and economic *karma* function. But the function was determined by its suitability to the type and its helpfulness the discipline; it was not the primary or sole factor." The features of the six stages as described by Sri Aurobindo from Indian and universal perspective are given in the Table 4.2 below:

Table 4.2

Psychological Stage	Characteristics
Symbolic	Predominantly religious and spiritual. The other elements, psychological, ethical, economic, physical are there but subordinated to the spiritual and religious ideas.*
Typal	Predominantly psychological and ethical; all else, even the religious, is subordinated to the psychological idea and to the ethical ideal which expresses it. Religion becomes then a mystic sanction for the ethical motive and discipline, Dharma; that becomes its chief social utility and for the rest it takes a more and more other worldly turn. The idea of the direct expression of the divine being or cosmic principle in man ceases to dominate or to be the leader and in the forefront; it recedes, stands in the background and finally disappears from the practice and in the end even from the theory of life.*
	This typal stage creates the great social ideals which remain impressed upon the human mind even when the stage itself is passed.*

Contd...

Contd...

Psychological Stage	Characteristics
Conventional	The conventional stage of human society is born when the external supports, the outward expressions of the spirit or the ideal become more important than the ideal, the body or even the clothes more important than the person. The tendency of the conventional age of the society is to fix, to arrange firmly, to stereotype religion, to bind education and training to traditional and unchangeable form, to subject thought to infallible authorities, to cast a stamp of finality on what seems to it the finished life of man. Always the form prevails and the spirit recedes.*
Individualistic	There arrives a period when the gulf between the convention and the truth becomes intolerable and the men of intellectual power arise, the great 'swallowers of formulas', who rejecting robustly or fiercely or with the calm light of reason symbol and type and convention, strike at the walls of the prison-house and seek by the individual reason, moral sense or emotional desire the Truth that society has lost or buried in its whited sepulchres. It is then that the individualistic age of religion and thought and society is created; the Age of Protestantism has begun, the Age of Reason, the Age of Revolt, Progress, Freedom.*
Subjective	To find the truth of things and the law of his being in relation to that truth man must go deeper and fathom the subjective secret of himself and things as well as their objective forms and surroundings. A necessary passage to the subjective period of humanity through which man has to circle back towards the recovery of his deeper self and a new upward line or a new revolving cycle of civilisation.*

* Extracts from Sri Aurobindo's work, *The Human Cycles*.

BARBARISM AND CIVILIZATION

Characteristics of Barbarism

The man in Barbaric stage lived like animal. He was driven by animal instinct and fulfilled his needs driven by the biological motive forces of self-existence and self-propagation, food and sex, and manifested the following traits. The man in Barbaric stage:

- is a creature of the environment and lives like an animal,
- moves in search of food just like any animal,
- is driven by the biological motive forces of self-existence and self-propagation, food and sex,
- is not mentally developed,
- has little sense of family life, religion and culture,
- has neither social manners nor moral principles as his faculties are not developed.

Characteristics of Civilization

In the evolutionary process, life evolved from matter and from life arose mind with the rise of man, *Homo sapiens*. Man became conscious of himself and the surrounding world. He utilised his mind to find solution to life's problems which he encountered in his day-to-day living process. Thus man, the thinker of Nature, ushered the psycho-social phase of evolution and gave birth to human civilizations. The civilized life developed after many years of struggle, search and research on problems around. "In its ordinary, popular sense, civilisation means", says Sri Aurobindo, "the state of civil society, governed, policed, organised, educated, possessed of knowledge and appliances as opposed to that which has not or is not supposed to have these advantages".

EXTRACTS FROM SRI AUROBINDO'S WORK, *THE HUMAN CYCLE*

Barbarism and Civilisation

According to Sri Aurobindo—Barbarism is the state of society in which man is almost entirely preoccupied with his life and body, his economic and physical existence—at first with their sufficient maintenance, not as yet their greater or richer well-being, and has few means and little inclination to develop his mentality, while civilisation is the more evolved state of society in which a sufficient social and economic organisation is added, the activity of the mental life in most if not all of its parts; for sometimes some of these parts are left aside or discouraged or temporarily atrophied by their inactivity, yet the society may be very obviously civilised and even highly civilised. This conception will bring in all the civilisations, historic and prehistoric and put aside all the barbarism, whether of Africa or Europe or Asia, Hun or Goth or Vandal or Turcoman. It is obvious that in a state of barbarism the rude beginnings of civilisation may exist; it is obvious too that in a civilised society a great mass of barbarism or numerous relics of it may exist.

In that sense all societies are semi-civilised. How much of our present day civilisation will be looked back upon with wonder and disgust by a more developed humanity as the superstitions and atrocities of an imperfectly civilised era. But the main point is that in any society which we can call civilised, the mentality of man must be active, the mental pursuits developed and the regulation and the improvement of his life by the mental being a clearly self-conscious concept in his better mind.

But in a civilised society there is still the distinction between the partially, crudely, conventionally civilised and the cultured. It would seem therefore, that the mere participation in the ordinary benefits of civilisation is not enough to raise a man into the mental life properly; a farther development, a higher elevation is needed. The last generation drew emphatically the distinction between the cultured man and the Philistine and got a fairly clear idea of what was meant by it. Roughly, the Philistine was for them the man who lives outwardly the civilised life, possesses all its paraphernalia, has and mouths the current stock of opinions, prejudices, conventions, sentiments, but is impervious to ideas, exercises no free intelligence, is innocent of beauty and art, vulgarises everything that he touches, religion, ethics, literature or life.

The Philistine is in fact the modern civilised barbarian, he is often the half-civilised physical and vital barbarian by his unintelligent attachment to the life of the body, the life of the vital needs and impulses and the ideal of the merely domestic and economic human animal; but essentially and commonly he is the mental barbarian, the average sensational man. That is to say, his mental life is that of the lower substratum of the mind, the life of the senses, the life of the sensations, the life of the emotions, the life of practical conduct—the first status of the mental being. In all these he may be very active, very vigorous, but he does not govern them by a higher light or seek to uplift them to a freer and nobler eminence, rather he pulls the higher faculties down to the level of his senses, his sensations, his enlightened and unchastened emotions, his gross utilitarian practicality. His aesthetic side is little developed.... His ethical bent is a habit of the sense-mind; it is the morality of the average sensational man.... He is not mentally active, but mentally reactive.

Civilisation can never be safe so long as, confining the cultured mentality to a small minority, it nourishes in its bosom a tremendous mass of ignorance, a multitude, a proletariat. Either knowledge must enlarge itself from above or be always in danger of submergence by the ignorant night from below. Still more must it be unsafe, if it allows enormous numbers of men to exist outside its pale uninformed by its light, full of the natural vigour of the barbarian, who may at any moment seize upon the physical weapons of the civilised without undergoing an intellectual transformation by their culture. The Graeco-Roman culture perished from within and from without, from without by the floods of Teutonic barbarism, from within by the loss of vitality. It gave the proletariat some measure of comfort and, amusement, but did not raise it into the light. When light came to the masses, it was from outside in the form of Christian religion which arrived as an enemy of the old culture.

Knowledge must be aggressive, if it wishes to survive and perpetuate itself; to leave an extensive ignorance either below or around it, is to expose humanity to the perpetual danger of a barbaric relapse.

Developed versus Cultured Nation or Age

Even when a nation or an age has developed within itself knowledge, science and arts, but still in its general outlook, its habit of life and thought is content to be governed not by knowledge, truth, beauty and high ideals of living, but by the gross vital, commercial, economic view of existence. We say that nation or age may be civilized in a sense, but for all its abundant and redundant appliances and apparatus of civilization it is not the realisation or the promise of a cultured humanity. Therefore, upon even the European civilization of the nineteenth century with all its triumphant and teeming production, its great developments of science, its achievement in the works of intellect, we pass a certain condemnation, because it has turned all these things to commercialism and to gross uses of vitalistic success.

We may say of it that this was not the perfection to which humanity ought to aspire and that this trend travels away from and not towards the higher curve of human evolution. It must be our definite verdict upon it that it was inferior as an age of culture to ancient Athens, to Italy of the Renaissance, to ancient or classical India. For great as might be the deficiencies of social organisation in those eras and though their range of scientific knowledge and material achievement was immensely inferior, yet they were more advanced in the art of life, knew better its objects and aimed more powerfully at some clear ideal of human perfection.

Not to live principally in the activities of the sense-mind, but in the activities of knowledge and reason and a wide intellectual curiosity, the activities of the enlightened will make the character and high ethical ideals and a large human action, not to be governed by our lower or average mentality but by truth and beauty and the self-ruling will is the ideal of a true culture and the beginning of an accomplished humanity.

FUTURE SOCIETY

"The Phenomenon of Modern Social Development" wrote Sri Aurobindo in his *Treaties, War and Self Determination*, "is the decline of the Brahmin and Kshatriya, of the Church, the military aristocracy and the aristocracy of letters and culture, and the rise to power or predominance of the commercial and industrial classes, Vaishya and Shudra, capital and labour. Together they have swallowed up or cast out their rivals and are now engaged in a fatricidal conflict for sole possession in which the completion of the downward force of social gravitation, the ultimate triumph of labour and the remodelling of all social conceptions and institutions with labour as the first, the most dignified term which will give its value to all others seem to be the visible writing of Fate. At present, however, it is the Vaishya who still predominates and his stamp on the world in commercialism, the predominance of the economic man, the universality of the commercial value or the utilitarian and materially efficient and productive value for everything in human life. Even in the outlook on knowledge, thought, science, art, poetry and religion the economic conception of life overrides all others".

In the psycho-social phase of evolution every human being is potentially *a jnana-kriya dhara*, upholder of knowledge and action. Only the highly evolved human beings with free intelligence can work in freedom for truth and universal well-being, they are in true sense Brahmins. They never depend upon anybody for any thing. The intelligentia, especially the scientists and technologists may be considered as the *Brahmins* of the modern age. But the big question mark is how many of them are endowed with free intelligence and work in freedom for truth and universal well-being? Do they depend on themselves for everything or influenced or directed by the funding agencies?

The Trends of Present Modernisation Process

The present Society is rapidly changing due to new knowledge and new needs of our times. It is going through 'modernization process' which is characterized by the following six factors:

- Urbanization
- Industrialization
- Mobilization
- Democratization
- Institutionalization
- Globalization.

Urbanization

There is a rapid growth of towns and cities due to many facilities available for people such as electricity, transport, communication, municipal services and more and better opportunities for comfortable life. More and more people are leaving rural areas and settling in cities and town to enjoy better standards of living.

Industrialization

All countries have gone through industrial revolution due to scientific inventions and new tools of technology. More employment opportunities are available in industries in cities for both skilled and unskilled workers. Industries provide scope for division of labour and so each worker does a specialized job in factories. There is scope for well-organized life among workers who get maximum benefit and full satisfaction in life.

Mobilization

There are many easy means of transport and communication available so that modern man is able to enjoy geographical and social mobility these days. He is no more a 'stay at home' person of the past but a 'man-on-move' of the present modern age.

Democratization

Almost all the civilized nations have organized themselves on democratic principles of freedom, equality and justice. Hence, modern man is able to exercise his rights and do his duties as well as responsibilities as citizen. He participates in making laws and elects his choicest Government. He can change the Government, if it is dysfunctional. Democracy is the key to modernization and civilization of today.

Institutionalization

In every civilized society, there are many organized institutions for the welfare and progress of individuals in all the spheres. Family, School, College, University, Church, Bank, Government, Unions, Federations and Professional/Commercial groups are some of the examples. The modern man has been able to live a civilized life and has attained peace, progress and prosperity.

Globalization

The modern societies of today are globally connected and interdependent. No society can remain isolated today because easy means of transport and communication are available now-a-days. Besides, all the nations are committed to global co-operation for common problems. For example, war on terrorism started by the United State in Afghanistan had a global support and sanction. Due to these factors and forces, all the societies in future will feel the need of the following:

- Need for adjustment with rapid changes in human life.
- Need for human values for survival.
- Need for scientific temper and rational outlook.
- Need for co-existence and global co-operation.
- Need for integration of Multicultural, Mutiracial and Multilingual societies in every country.

Components of Modernization

Future society will be in constant and continuous process of modernization, which means the society has to readjust itself to new demands of time and new challenges of survival. It calls for new changes, new goals and new institutions to achieve the results. Some experts of social sciences have analysed the concept of modernization and have given ten components of the process:

- Empathy for fellow beings.
- Mobility, social and economic.
- Active participation in social institutions.
- Interest aggregation and interest articulation.
- Achievement orientation.
- Rational ends-means calculation.
- New attitudes to wealth, work and savings.
- Faith in desirability and possibility of change.
- Social, economic and political discipline.
- Capacity to put off immediate short term gains for the long-term higher gains in future.

Thus, modernization is the "total transformation" of a traditional society into the updated society with scientific knowledge and technological tools, advanced economy and political stability.

Adaptive Demands

For modernization, every traditional society has to fulfil the needs of transformation and adapt itself to the new demands of the new scientific age. Some educationists have analysed these areas in which these demands are to be met. They are as follows:

- In political sphere, new system of representative Government, political parties and civil services is to be created.
- In educational sphere, new system of mass literacy, equal educational opportunities and vocational skill-based programmes of training and education is to be developed.
- In social sphere, open tolerant society of multiracial, multilingual and multicultural groups is to be accepted.
- In economic sphere, new approaches of production and distribution system are to be adopted for the welfare of all citizens.
- In religious sphere, secular and rational outlook along with mutual tolerance for different beliefs or faiths is to be developed.

EXTRACT FROM SRI AUROBINDO'S WORK, *THE HUMAN CYCLE*

The Curve of the Rational Age

Sri Aurobindo explains "It has been an age of progress; but progress is of two kinds, adaptive, with a secure basis in an unalterable social principle and constant change only in the circumstances and machinery of its application to suit fresh ideas and fresh needs, or else radical, with no long-secure basis, but instead a constant root questioning of the practical foundations and even the central principle of the established society. The modern age has resolved itself into a constant series of radical progression.

If we may judge from the modern movement, the progress of the reason as a social renovator and creator, if not interrupted in its course, would be destined to pass through three successive stages, which are the very logic of its growth, the first individualistic and increasingly democratic with liberty for its principle, the second socialistic, in the end perhaps a governmental communism with equality and the State for its principle, the third—if that ever gets beyond the stage of theory—anarchistic in the higher sense of that much-abused word, either a loose voluntary co-operation or a free communalism with brotherhood or comradeship and not government for its principle.

Man, the half infra-rational being, demands three things for his satisfaction, power, if he can have it, but at any rate the use and reward of his faculties and the enjoyment of his desires. In the old societies the possibility of these could be secured by him to a certain extent according to his birth, his fixed status and the use of his capacity within the limits of his hereditary status. That basis once removed and no proper substitute provided, the same ends can only be secured by success in a scramble for the one power left, the power of wealth. Accordingly, instead of a harmoniously ordered society there has developed a huge organised competitive system, a frantically rapid and one-sided development of industrialism and, under the garb of democracy, an increasing plutocratic tendency that shocks by its ostentatious grossness and the magnitudes of its gulfs and distances. These have been the last results of the individualistic machinery, the initial bankruptcies of the rational age".

"The business of the reason is intermediate: it is to observe and understand this life by the intelligence and discover for it the direction in which it is going and the laws of its self-development on the way. In order that it may do its office, it is oblised to adopt temporarily fixed view-points none of which is more than partially true and to create systems none of which can really stand as the final expression of the integral truth of things. The integral truth of things is truth not of the reason but of the spirit."

- In technological sphere, new tools and techniques for workers in every field are to be applied for more production in society.
- In family sphere, nuclear families with limited children and small size is to be accepted and propagated for population control.
- In administrative sphere, an accountable, fair and just management system is to be developed.
- In moral sphere, necessary human values are to be cultivated to promote love and fellowship among citizens of the world.
- In international sphere, concept of interdependence, unity and co-operation is to be promoted for progress and prosperity of all nations.

Future of Indian Society

India, one of the oldest civilisations extant on earth, and as a developing country, in modern terminology has to renovate the society by making need-based rapid changes in all the spheres mentioned above. It has to resolve all types of crises in social, economic, political, environmental, educational and moral spheres to be a leading nation in the world.

Human society is passing through a great transition. The mechanistic world view of the classical physics based on the mathematical theory of Newton, the philosophy of Descartes and the scientific methodology advocated by Bacon dominated world development during seventeenth, eighteenth and nineteenth centuries. Several conceptual revolutions witnessed in the twentieth century. Physics revealed the limitations of the mechanistic world view. It has resulted in the emergence of an organic ecological world view akin to the mystic world views of all ages and traditions. For sustainable development human society is progressing towards a solar age culture.

The evolution of a society—structural, economic, political, cultural, religious, environmental—is influenced by the continuity or changes in the value system. There are certain values which are eternal and in harmony with the laws that govern Nature and the inner foundations of beings which should determine the future course of development and progress. India has to take into account the conflicting forces of development in the world as well as the impact of changes in the conceptual world, view and play her historical role as a great synthesiser. The 21st Century offers both the challenges and the opportunities for the Indian sub-continent to be a developed nation by 2020. It will be possible only through a total commitment of people to build New India of Gandhiji's dreams.

Lifelong Education for Future

The International Commission on the Development of Education was appointed to recommend to the world body like UNESCO, the suggestions for solving the problems of education along with suitable means, media, strategies and reflections. The report produced by the Commission not only has dealt with problems of the international community of interest in education, but also emphasized the gap which is widening between the developed and the developing countries in a very striking way. While presenting the report, its Chairman Edgare Faure (1973) has mentioned the four basic assumptions underlying it.

The first, which is indeed the justification for the task, the Commission undertook as that of the existence of an international community which amidst the variety of nations and cultures, of political options and degrees of development, is reflected in common aspirations, problems and trends and in its movement towards one and the same destiny. The corollary to this is the fundamental solidarity of Governments and of peoples, despite transitory differences and conflicts. *The second* is belief in democracy, conceived of as implying each man's right to realize his own potential and to share in the building of his own future. The keystone of democracy so conceived is education—not only education that is accessible to all, but education whose aims and methods have been thought out afresh. *The third* assumption is that the aim of development is the complete fulfillment of man, in all the richness of his personality, the complexity of his forms, of expression and his various commitments—as individual, member of family, and of a community, citizen and producer, inventor of techniques and creative dreamer. *The last* assumption is that only an overall lifelong education can produce the kind of complete man, the need for whom is increasing with the continually more stringent constraints tearing the individual asunder. We should no longer assiduously acquire knowledge once and for all, but learn how to build-up a continuously evolving body of knowledge all through lifelong education.

Ideals and Philosophy of Indian Society

5

Ideals are truths that have not yet effected themselves for man, the realities of a higher plane of existence which have yet to fulfil themselves on this lower plane of life and matter, our present field of operation. To the pragmatical intellect which takes its stand upon the ever-changing present, ideals are not truths, not realities, they are at most potentialities of future truth and only become real when they are visible in the external fact as work of force accomplished. But to the mind, which is able to draw back from the flux of force in the material universe, to the consciousness which is not imprisoned in its own workings or carried along in their flood but is able to envelop, hold and comprehend them, to the soul that is not merely the subject and instrument of the world-force but can reflect something of that Master-Consciousness which controls and uses it, the ideal present to its inner vision is a greater reality than the changing fact, obvious to its outer senses. The Idea is not a reflection of the external fact which it so much exceeds; rather the fact is only a partial reflection of the Idea which has created it.

Certainly, ideals are not the ultimate Reality, for that is too high and vast for any ideal to envisage; they are aspects of it thrown out in the world-consciousness as a basis for the working of the world-power. But they are primary, the actual workings secondary. They are nearer to the Reality and therefore always more real, forcible and complete than the facts which are their partial reflection. Reflections themselves of the Real, they again are reflected in the more concrete workings of our existence.

The human intellect, in proportion as it limits itself by the phenomena of self-realising force, fails to catch the creative idea until after we have seen the external fact it has created; but this order of our sense-enslaved consciousness is not the real order of the universe. God pre-exists before the world can come into being, but to our experience in which the senses act first and only then the finer workings of consciousness, the world seems to come first and God to emerge out of it, so much so that it costs us an effort to rise out of the mechanical, pluralistic and pantheistic conceptions of Him to a truer and higher idea of the Divine Reality. That which to us is the ultimate, is in truth the primary reality. So, too, the idea which seems to us to rise out of the fact, really precedes it and out of it the fact has arisen. Our vulgar contrast of the ideal and the real is therefore a sensuous error, for that which we call real is only a phenomenon of force working out something that stands behind the phenomenon and that is pre-existent and greater than it. The Real, the idea, the phenomenon, this is the true order of the creative Divinity.

The pragmatic intellect is only sure of a thing when it finds it realised in Power; therefore it has a certain contempt for the ideal, for the vision, because it drives always at execution and material realisation. But Power is not the only term of the Godhead; Knowledge is the elder sister of Power Force and Consciousness are twin aspects of being, both in the eternal foundation of things and in their evolutionary realisation.

The idea is the realisation of a truth in Consciousness as the fact is its realisation in Power, both indispensable, both justified in themselves and in each other, neither warranted in ignoring or despising its complement. For the idealist and visionary to despise, the pragmatist or for the pragmatist to depreciate the idealist and visionary, is a deplorable result of our intellectual limitations and the mutual misunderstandings by which the arrogance of our imperfect temperament and mentality shuts itself out from perfection. It is as if we were to think that God the Seer and Knower must despise. God the Master of works and energies or the Lord of action and sacrifice ignore the divine Witness and Originator. But these two are one and the division in us a limitation that mankind has yet to conquer.

Human being advances in proportion as he becomes more and more capable of knowing before he realises in action. This is indeed the order of evolution. It begins with a material working in which the Prakriti, the executive Power, is veiled by its works, by the facts it produces, and itself veils the consciousness which originates and supports all its workings. In life the force emerges and becomes vibrant in the very surface of its works, last, in mind the underlying consciousness reveals itself. So, too, man is at first subject in his mentality to the facts which his senses envisage, cannot go behind and beyond them, knows only the impressions they make on his receptive mind. The animal is executive, not creative; a passive tool of Matter and Life, he does not seek in his thought and will to react upon and use them: the human being too, in his less developed state is executive rather than creative; he limits his view to the present and to his environment, works so as to live from day to day, accepts what he is without reaching forward in thought to what he may be, has no ideals. In proportion, as he goes beyond the fact and seeks to anticipate Nature, to catch the ideas and principles behind his workings and finally to seize the idea that is not yet realised infact and himself preside over its execution, he becomes originative and creative and no longer merely executive. He begins thus, his passage from subjection to mastery.

Thus, progressing humanity falls apart after its fashion into classes; it divides itself between the practical man and the idealist man and makes numerous compromises between the two extremes. In reality the division is artificial; for every man who does anything in the world, works by virtue of an idea and in the force given to him by ideals, either his own or other's ideals, which he may or may not recognise but in whose absence nevertheless he would be impotent to move a single step.

It cannot be doubted which of these two opposites and complementaries is the most essential to success. Not only is the upheaval and fertilising of the general consciousness by the thinker and the idealist essential to the practical realisation of great changes, but in the realisation itself the idealist who will not compromise is an indispensable element. The age or the country which is entirely composed of reasonable statesman like workers ever ready for concession and compromise is a country which will never be great until it has added to itself what is lacking to it and bathed itself in pure and divine fountains and an age which will accomplish nothing of supreme importance for the progress of humanity.

There is a difference, however, between the fanatic of an idea and the true idealist. The former is simply the materialistic, executive man possessed by the idea of another, not himself the possessor of it; he is haunted in his will and driven by the force of the idea, not really illumined by its light. He does harm as well as good and his chief use is to prevent the man of compromise from pausing at a paltry or abortive result, but his excesses also bring about great reactions. Incapable of taking his stand on the ideal itself, he puts all his emphasis on particular means and forms and overstrains the springs of action till they become dulled and incapable of responding to further excitation. But the true idealist is not the servant of the letter or the form; it is the idea which he loves and the spirit behind the idea which he serves.

Man approaches nearer his perfection when he combines in himself the idealist and the pragmatist, the originative soul and the executive power. Great executive personalities have usually been men of a considerable idealism. But the greatest men of action who were endowed by Nature with the most extraordinary force of accomplishment, have owed it to the combination in them of active power with an immense drift of originative thought devoted to practical realisation. They have been great executive thinkers, great practical dreamers. Such were Napoleon and Alexander. Napoleon with his violent prejudice against ideologues and dreamers, was himself a colossal dreamer, an incurable if unconscious ideologist; his teeming brain was the cause of his gigantic force and accomplishment. The immense if shapeless ideas of Alexander threw themselves into the form of conquests, cities, cultures;

they broke down the bafflers of Greek and Asiatic prejudice and narrow self-imprisonment and created an age of civilisation and soul-interchange.

But these great personalities do not contain in themselves the combination which humanity most needs; not the man of action driven by ideas, the pragmatist stirred by a half-conscious exaltation from the idealistic, almost the mystic side of his nature, but the seer who is able to execute his vision is the higher term of human power and knowledge. One takes his stand in the *Prakriti*, the executive force, and is therefore rather driven than leads himself even when he most successfully leads others; the other takes his stand in the *Purusha*, the knower who controls executive force, and he possesses the power that he uses. He draws nearer to the type of the divine Seer-Will that as created and governs the universe. But such a combination is rare and difficult; for in order to grasp the ideal, the human soul has to draw back so far from the limitations, pettiness, denials of the world of phenomenal fact that the temperament and mentality become inapt for executive action upon the concrete phenomena of life and matter. The mastery of the fact is usually possible to the idealist mind only when its idealism is of no great depth or power and can therefore, accommodate itself more easily to the actual life-environment.

Until this difficulty is overcome and the Seer-Will becomes more common in man and more the master of life, the ideal works at a disadvantage, by a silent pressure upon the reluctant world, by occasional attacks and sudden upheavals; a little is accomplished in a long time or by a great and sudden effort, a little that is poor enough, coarse enough, material enough compared with the thing seen and attempted, but which still makes a farther advance possible though often after a period of quiescence and reaction.

And times there are, ages of stupendous effort and initiative when the gods seem no longer satisfied with this tardy and fragmentary working, when the ideal breaks constantly through the dull walls of the material practical life, incalculable forces clash in its field, innumerable ideas meet and wrestle in the arena of the world and through the constant storm and flash, agitation of force and agitation of light, the possibility of the victoriously fulfilled ideal, the hope of the Messiah, the expectation of the Avatar takes possession of the hearts and thoughts of men. Such an age seems now to be coming upon the world. But whether that hope and expectation and possibility are to come to anything depends upon whether men prepare their souls for the advent and rise in the effort of their faith, life and thought to the height and purity of a clearly-grasped ideal. The Messiah or Avatar is nothing but this, the divine Seer-Will descending upon the human consciousness to reveal to it the divine meaning behind our half-blind action and to give along with the vision the exalted will that is faithful and performs and the ideal force that executes according to the vision.

Yoga and Skill in Works

Yoga, says the *Gita*, is skill in works, and by this phrase the ancient Scripture meant that the transformation of mind and being to which it gave the name of Yoga brought with it a perfect inner state and faculty out of which the right principle of action and the right spiritual and divine result of works emerged naturally like a tree out of its seed. Certainly, it did not mean that the clever general or politician or lawyer or shoemaker deserves the name of Yogin; it did not mean that any kind of skill in works was Yoga, but by Yoga it signified a spiritual condition of universal equality and God-union and by the skill of the Yogic worker it intended a perfect adaptation of the soul and its instruments to the rhythm of the divine and universal *Prakriti* liberated from the shackles of egoism and the limitations of the sense-mind.

Essentially, Yoga is a generic name for the processes and the result of processes by which we transcend or shred off our present modes of being and rise to a new, a higher, a wider mode of consciousness which is not that of the ordinary animal and intellectual man. Yoga is the exchange of an egoistic for a universal or cosmic consciousness lifted towards or informed by the super-cosmic, transcendent unnameable who is the source and support of all things.

Yoga is the passage of the human thinking animal towards the God consciousness from which he has descended. In that ascent we find many levels and stages, plateau after plateau of the hill whose summit touches truth of things; but at every stage the saying of the *Gita* applies in an ever higher degree. Even a little of this new law and inner order delivers the soul out of the great peril by which it had been overtaken in its world-ward descent, the peril of the ignorance by which the unillumined intellect even when it is keenest or sagest must ever be bound and limited, of the sorrow and sin from which the unpurified heart, even when it wears the richest purple of aspiration and feeling, must ever suffer soil and wound and poverty, and of the vanity of its works to which the undivinised will of man, even when it is most vehement and powerful or Olympian and victorious, must eternally be subject. It is the utility of Yoga that it opens to us a gate of escape out of the vicious circle of our ordinary human existence.

The idea of works, in the thought of the *Gita*, is the widest possible. All action of Nature in man is included, whether it be internal or external, operate in the mind or use the body, seem great or seem little. From the toil of the hero to the toil of the cobbler, form the labour of the sage to the simple physical act of eating, all is included. The seeking of the Self by thought, the adoration of the highest by the emotions of the heart, the gathering of means and material and capacity and the use of them for the service of God and man, stand here on an equal footing. Buddha sitting under the Bo-tree and conquering the illumination, the ascetic silent and motionless in his cave, Shankara storming through India debating with all men and preaching most actively the gospel of inaction are all from this point of view doing great and forceful work. But while the outward action may be the same, there is great internal difference between the working of the ordinary man and the working of the Yogin, a difference in the state of the being, a difference in the power and the faculty, a difference in the will and temperament.

What we do, arises out of what we are. The existent is conscious of what he is; that consciousness formulates itself as knowledge and power; works are the result of this two-fold force of being in action. Mind, life and body can only operate out of that which is contained in the being of which they are forces. This is what we mean when we say that all things act according to their nature.

The divine Existence is pure and unlimited being in possession of all itself, it is *sat*; whatever it puts forth in its limitless purity of self-awareness is truth of itself *satya*; the divine knowledge is knowledge of the Truth, the divine Will is power of the Truth, the divine workings are words and ideas of the Truth realising themselves in manifold forms and through many stages and in infinite relations. But God is not limited or bound by any particular working or any moment of time or any field of space or any law of relation, because He is universal and infinite. Nor is He limited by the universe; for His infinity is not cosmic, but supracosmic.

But the individualised being is or acts as if he were so bound and limited, because he treats the particular working of existence that he is and the particular moment of time and field of space in which it is actually operating and the particular conditions which reign in the working and in the moment and in the field as if they were self-existent realities and the binding truth of things. Himself his knowledge, his force and will, his relations with the world and his fellows, his need in it and his desire from them he treats as the sufficient truth and reality, the point of departure of all his works, the central fact and law of his universe. And from this egoistic error arises an all-vitiating falsehood. For the particular, the individual can have no self-existence, no truth, no valid force except in so far as it reflects rightly and relates and conforms itself justly to the universal, to the all-being, the all-knowledge, the all-will and follows its true drift towards self-realisation and vast delight in itself. Therefore, the salvation of the individual lies in his universalising himself; and this is the lesson which life tries always to teach him, but the obstinate ego is always unwilling to learn; for the universal is not any group or extended ego, not the family, community, nation or even all mankind, but an infinite far surpassing all these littlenesses.

Nor is the universalising of himself sufficient for liberation, although certainly it will make him practically more free and in his being nearer to the true freedom. To put himself in tune with the universal is a step, but beyond the universal and directing and determining it is the supra-cosmic infinity, for the universe also has no self-existence, truth or validity except as it expresses the divine Being, Knowledge, Will, Power, Delight of Him who surpasses all universe, so much that it can be said figuratively that with a petty fragment of His being and a single ray of His consciousness.

He has created all these worlds. Therefore, the universalised mind must look up from its cosmic consciousness to the Supernal and derive from that all its sense of being and movement of works. This is the fundamental truth from which the Yogic consciousness starts; it helps the individual to universalise himself and then to transcend the cosmic formula. And this transformation acts not only on his status of being but on his active consciousness in works.

The *Gita* tells us that equality of soul and mind is Yoga and that this equality is the foundation of the Brahman-state, that high infinite consciousness to which the Yogin aspires. Now equality of mind means universality; for without universality of soul there may be a state of indifference or an impartial self-control or a well-governed equality of temperament, but these are not the thing that is meant. The equality spoken of is not indifference or impartiality or equability, but a fundamental oneness of attitude to all persons and all things and happenings because of the perception of all as the One. Such equality, it is erroneously thought, is incompatible with action. By no means; this is the error of the animal and the intellectual man who thinks that action is solely possible when dictated by his hopes, fears and passions or by the self-willed preferences of the emotion and the intellect justifying themselves by the illusions of the reason. That might be the fact if the individual were the real actor and not merely an instrument or secondary agent; but we know well enough, for science and philosophy assure us of the same truth, that the universal is the Force which acts through the simulacrum of our individuality.

The individual mind, pretending to choose for itself with a sublime ignorance and disregard of the universal, is obviously working on the basis of a falsehood and by means of an error and not in the knowledge and the will of the Truth. It cannot have any real skill in works: for to start from a falsehood or half-truth and work by means of blunders and arrive at another falsehood or half-truth which we have immediately to change, and all the while to weep and struggle and suffer and have no sure resting-place, cannot surely be called skill in works. But the universal is equal in all and therefore, its determinations are not self-willed preferences but are guided by the truth of the divine will and knowledge which is unlimited and not subject to incapacity or error.

Therefore, the state of his being by which the Yogin differs from the ordinary man, is that by which he rises from the foundation of a perfect equality to the consciousness of the one existence in all and embracing all and lives in that existence and not in the walls of his body or personal temperament or limited mind. Mind, life and body he sees as small enough things which happen and change and develop in his being. Nay, the whole universe is seen by him as happening within himself, not in his small ego or mind, but within this vast and infinite self with which he is now constantly identified. All actions in the universe he sees as arising in this being, out of the divine Existence and under the stress of the divine Truth, Knowledge, Will and Power. He beings to participate consciously in its working and to see all things in the light of that divine truth and governance; and even when his own action move on certain lines rather than other, he is not bound by them or shut to the truth of all the rest by his own passions and preferences, groupings and seeking and revolts.

It is evident that such an increasing wideness revolts. It is evident that such an increasing wideness or vision must mean an increasing wideness of vision, must mean an increasing knowledge. To use the figures of the Vedic seers, by Yoga, *Varuna* is born in us, a vast sky of spiritual living, the Divine in his wide existence and infinite truth; into that wideness *Mitra* rises up, Lord of Light and love who takes all our activities of thought, feelings and will, links them into a Divine harmony, charioteers, our movement and dictates our works; called by this wideness and this harmony Aryaman appears in us, the Divine in its illumined power, uplifted force of being and all-judging effective will; and by the three, comes the indwelling *Bhaga*, the Divine in its pure bliss and all-seizing joy who dispels the evil dream of our jarring and divided existence and possesses all things in the light and glory of *Aryamn's* power, *Mitra's* love and light, *Varuna's* unity. This divine Birth shall be the son of our works; and then creating this, what greater skill can there be or what more practical and sovereign cunning?

Conservation and Progress

Mankind thinks naturally in extremes or else reconciles by a patchwork and compromise. Whether he makes a fetish of moderation or surrenders himself to the enthusiasm of the single idea, the human being misses always truth of vision and the right pitch of action because instead of seeing, feeling and becoming in obedience to his nature like other animate existences he tries always to measure things by a standard he has set up in his intelligence. The human mind is strong and swift in analysis; it synthesises with labour imperfectly and does not feel at home in its synthesis. It divides, opposes and placed between the oppositions, it creates, becomes an eager partisan of one side or another; but to think wisely and impartially and with a certain totality is irksome and disgusting to the normal human being.

All human action as all human thought suffers from these disabilities. This characteristic of human mentality show itself in the opposition we create between conservation and progress. Nothing in the universe can really stand still because everything there is a mould of Time and the very essence of Time is change by a movement forward. As for standing still, it is an impossibility, a delusion, a fiction. Only the spirit is stable; the soul and body of things are in eternal motion. And in this motion there are the three determining powers of the past, future and present.

The past is both a drag and a force for progress. It is all that has created the present and a great part of the force that is creating the future. For the past is not dead; its forms are gone and had to go, otherwise the present would not have come into being: but its soul, its power, its essence lives veiled in the present and ever-accumulating, growing, deepening will live on in the future. Every human being holds in and behind him all the past of his own race, of humanity and of himself; these three things determine his starting point and pursue him through his life's progress.

It is in the force of this past, in the strength which its huge conservation's give to him that he confronts the unillumined abysses of the future and plunges forward into the depths of its unrealised infinities. But also it is a drag, partly because man afraid of the unknown clings to the old forms of which he is sure, the old foundations which feel so safe under his feet, the old props around which so many of his attachments and associations cast their tenacious tendrils, but also partly because the forces of the past keep their careful hold on him so as to restrain him in his uncertain course and prevent the progress from becoming a precipitation.

The future repels us even while it irresistibly attracts. The future is a sphinx with two minds, an energy which offers itself and denies, gives itself and resists, seeks to enthrone us and seeks to slay. But the conquest has to be attempted, the wager has to be accepted. We have to face the future's offer of death as well as its offer of life, and it need not alarm us, for it is by constant death to our old names and forms that we shall live most vitally in greater and newer forms and names. Go on we must; for if we do not, Time itself will force us forward in spite of our fancied immobility. The greatest spirits are therefore those who have no fear of the future, who accept its challenge and its wager: they have that sublime trust in the God or Power that guides the world, that high audacity of the human soul to wrestle with the infinite and realise the impossible, that wise and warrior confidence in its ultimate destiny which marks the Avatars and Prophets and great innovators and renovators.

If we consider carefully, we shall see that the past is indeed a huge force of conservation, but of conservation that is not immobile, that on the contrary offers itself as material for change and new realisation that the present is the constant change and new actual realisation which the past desires and compels; and that the future is that force of new realisation not yet actual towards which the past was moving and for the sake of which it lived. Then we perceive that there is no real opposition between these three; we see that they are part of a single movement, a sort of Trinity of Vishnu-Brahma-Maheshwara fulfilling by an inseparable action, the one Deity. Yet the human mind in its mania of division and opposition seeks to set them at strife and ranges humanity into various camps, the partisans of the past, the partisans of the present and the partisans of the future.

The partisans of the future call themselves the party of progress, the children of light and denounce the past as ignorant, evil, a mass of errors and abuses. The partisans of the present look with honour upon all progresses as an impious and abominable plunge into error, evil, degeneration and ruin for them is the culmination of humanity. The partisans of the past are of two kinds. The first admit the defects of the present but support it in so far as it still cherishes the principles of the high, perfect, faultless, adorable past, that golden age of the race of community. A second kind condemn the present root and branch as degenerate, hateful, horrible, vicious, accursed; they erect a past form as the hope of a humanity returning to the wisdom of its forefathers. And to such quarrels of children the intellectuals and the leaders of thought and faith lend the power of the specious or moving word and the striking idea and the emotional fervour or religious ardour which they conceive to be the very voice, light and force of Truth itself in its utter self-revelation.

The true thinker can dispense with the eclat which attaches to the leader of partisans. He will strive to see this great divine movement as a whole, to know in its large lines the divine intention and goal in it without seeking to fix arbitrarily its details: he will strive to understand the greatness and profound meaning of the past without attaching himself to its forms, for he knows that forms must change and only the formless endures and that the past can never be repeated, but only its essence preserved, its power, its soul of good and its massed impulse towards a greater self-fulfilment; he will accept the actual realisations of the present as a stage and nothing more keenly appreciates its defects, self-satisfied errors, presumptuous pretensions because these are the chief enemies of progress, but not ignoring the truth and good that it has gained; and he will sound the future to understand what the Divine in it is seeking to realise, not only at the present moment, not only in the next generation, but beyond, and for that he will speak, strive, if need be battle, since battle is the method still used by Nature in humanity, even while all the while he knows that there is more yet beyond beside which, when it comes to light, the truth he has seized will seem erroneous and limited. Therefore, he will act without presumption and egoism, knowing that his own errors and those which he combats are alike necessary forces in that labour and movement of human life towards the growing Truth and Good by which there increases shadowily the figure of a far-off divine Ideal.

The Conservative Mind and Eastern Progress

The arrival of a new radical idea in the minds of men is the sign of a great coming change in human life and society; it may be combated, the reaction of the old idea may triumph for a time, but the struggle never leaves either the thoughts and sentiments or the habits and institutions of the society as they were when it commenced. Whether it knows it or not, it has gone forward and the change is irretrievable.

The conservative mind is unwilling to recognise this law though it is observable throughout human history and we can easily cull examples with full hands from all ages and all climes. This is only seized by a few conspicuous landmarks, the evolution and end of Athenian democracy, the transition from the Roman republic to the empire, the emergence of feudal

Europe out of the ruins of Rome, the Christianisation of Europe, the Reformation and Renaissance together preparing a new society, the French Revolution, the present rapid movement towards a socialistic State and the replacing of competition by organised co-operation. Because our view of European history is chiefly political, we do not see the constant mutation of society and of thought in the same relief; but we can recognise two great cycles of change, one of the ancient races leading from the primitive ages to the cultured society of the Graeco-Roman world, the other from the semi-barbarism of feudal Christendom to the intellectual, materialistic and civilised society of modern times.

In the East, on the contrary, the great revolutions have been spiritual and cultural; the political and social changes, although they have been real and striking, if less profound than in Europe, fall into the shade and are apt to be overlooked; besides, this unobtrusiveness is increased by their want of relief, the slow subtlety of their process and instinctive persistence and reverence with which old names and formulas have been preserved while the thing itself was profoundly modified until its original sense remained only as a pious fiction. Thus Japan kept its sacrosanct Mikado as a cover for the change to an aristocratic and feudal government and has again brought him forward in modern times to cover and facilitate without too serious a shock the transition from a medieval form of society into the full flood of modernism.

In India the continued fiction of the ancient four-fold order of society based on spiritual idealism, social type, ethical discipline and economic function is still used to cover and justify the quite different, complex and chaotic order of caste which, while it still preserves some confused fragments of the old motives, is really founded upon birth, privilege, local custom and religious formalism. The evolution from one type of society to another so opposed to it in its psychological motives and real institutions without any apparent change of formula is one of the most curious phenomena in the social history of mankind and still awaits intelligent study.

It is more difficult but still possible to appreciate the working of an idea against all obstacles through many centuries; we can comprehend now, for instance, that we must seek the beginnings of the French Revolution, not in Rousseau or Mirabeau or the blundering of Louis XVI, but in movements which date back to the Capet and the Valois, while the precise fact which prepared its tremendous outbreak and victory and determined its form was the defeat of the Calvinistic reformation in France and the absolute triumph of the monarchical system over the nobility and the bourgeoisie in the reigns of Louis XIII and Louis XIV. That double victory determined the destruction of the monarchy in France, the downfall of the Church and, by the failure of the nobles to lead faithfully the liberal cause whether in religion or politics, the disappearance of aristocracy.

But Nature has still more subtle and disguised movements in her dealings with men by which she leads them to change without their knowing that they have changed. It is because she has employed chiefly this method in the vast masses of the East that the conservative habit of mind is so much stronger there than in the West. It is able to nourish the illusion that it has not changed, that it is immovably faithful to the ideas of remote forefathers, to their religion, their traditions, their institutions, their social ideals, that it has preserved either a divine or an animal immobility both in thought and in the routine of life and has been free from the human law of mutation by which man and his social organisations must either progress or degenerate but can in no case maintain themselves unchanged against the attack of Time.

Buddhism has come and gone and the Hindu still professes to belong to the Vedic religion held and practised by his Aryan forefathers; he calls his creed the Aryan Dharma, the eternal religion. It is only when we look close that we see the magnitude of the illusion. Buddha has gone out of India indeed, but Buddhism remains; it has stamped its giant impress on the spirit of the national religion, leaving the forms to be determined by the Tantricism with which itself had made alliance and some sort of fusion in its middle growth; what it destroyed no man has been able to restore, what it left no man has been able to destroy. As a matter of fact, the double cycle which India has described from the early Vedic times to India of Buddha and the philosophers and again from Buddha to the time of the European irruption was in its own way as vast in change in religious, social, cultural, even political and administrative as the double cycle of Europe; but because it preserved old names for new things, old formulas for new methods and old coverings for new institutions and because the change was always marked in the internal but quiet an unobtrusive in the external, we have been able to create and preserve the fiction of the unchanging East.

There has also been this result that while the European conservative has learned the law of change in human society, knows that he must move and quarrel with the progressist only over the right pace and the exact direction, the eastern or rather the Indian conservative still imagines that stability may be the true law of mortal being, practises a sort of Yogic asana on the flood of Time and because he does not move himself, thinks for he keeps his eyes shut and is not in the habit of watching the banks, that he can prevent the stream also from moving on.

This conservative principle has its advantages even as rapid progress has its vices and its perils. It helps towards the preservation of a fundamental continuity which makes for the longevity of civilisations and the persistence of what was valuable in humanity's past. So, in India, if religion has changed immensely its form and temperament, the religious spirit has been really eternal, the principle of spiritual discipline is the same as in the earliest times the fundamental spiritual truths have been preserved and even enriched in their contents and the very forms can all be traced back through their mutations to the seed of the *Veda*.

On the other hand, this habit of mind leads to the accumulation of a great mass of accretions which were once valuable but have lost their virtue and to the heaping up of dead forms and shibboleths which no longer correspond to any vital truth nor have any understood and helpful significance.

All this putrid waste of the past is held to be too sacred to be touched by any profane hand and yet it chokes up the streams of the national life or corrupts its waters. And if no successful process of purification takes place, a state of general ill-health in the social body supervenes in which the principle of conservation becomes the cause of dissolution.

The present era of the world is a stage of immense transformations. Not one but many radical ideas are at work in the mind of humanity and agitate its life with a vehement seeking and effort at change; and although the centre of the agitation is in progressive Europe, yet the East is being rapidly drawn into this churning of the sea of thought and this breaking up of old ideas and old institutions. No nation or community can any longer remain psychologically cloistered and apart in the unity of the modern world. It may even be said that the future of humanity depends most upon the answer that will be given to the modern riddle of the Sphinx by the East and especially by India, the hoary guardian of the Asiatic idea and its profound spiritual secrets. For the most vital issues of the age is whether the future progress of humanity is to be governed by the modern economic and materialistic mind of the West or by a nobler pragmatism guided, uplifted and enlightened by spiritual culture and knowledge.

The West never really succeeded in spiritualising itself and latterly it has been habituated almost exclusively to an action in the external governed by political and economic ideals and necessities; in spite of the reawakening of the religious mind and the growth of a widespread but not yet profound or luminous spiritual and psychical curiosity and seeking, it has to act solely in the things of this world and to solve its problems by mechanical methods and as the thinking political and economic animal, simply because it knows no other standpoint and is accustomed to no other method.

On the other hand the East, though it has allowed its spirituality to slumber too much in dead forms, has always been open to profound awakenings and preserves its spiritual capacity intact, even when it is actually inert and uncreative.

Therefore the hope of the world lies in the re-arousing in the East of the old spiritual practicality and large and profound vision and power of organisation under the insistent contact of the West and in the flooding but of the light of Asia on the Occident, no Longer in forms that are now static, effete, unadaptive, but in new forms stirred, dynamic and effective.

India, the heart of the Orient, has to change as the whole West and the whole East are changing, and it cannot avoid changing in the sense of the problems forced upon it by Europe. The new Orient must necessarily be the result either of some balance and fusion or of some ardent struggle between progressive and conservative ideals and tendencies. If therefore, the conservative mind in this counts opens itself sufficiently to the necessity of transformation, the resulting culture born of a resurgent India may well bring about a profound modification in the future civilisation of the world.

Our Indian Ideal

We believe in the constant progression of humanity and we hold that progression is the working out of a thought in Life which sometimes manifests itself on the surface and sometimes sinks below and works behind the mask of external forces and interests. When there is this lapse below the surface, humanity has its periods of apparent retrogression or tardy evolution, its long hours of darkness or twilight during which the secret Thought behind works out one of its phases by the pressure mainly of economic, political and personal interests ignorant of any deeper aim within. When the thought returns to the surface, humanity has its periods of light and of rapid efflorescence, its dawns and splendid spring tides, and according to the depth, vitality, truth and self-effective energy of the form of Thought that emerges is the importance of the stride forward that it makes during these Hours of the Gods in our terrestrial manifestation.

There is no greater error than to suppose, as the "practical" man is wont to do, that thought is only a fine flower and an ornament of life and that political, economic and personal interests are the important and effective motors of human action. We recognise that this is a world of life and action and developing organism; but the life that seeks to guide itself only by vital and material forces is a slow, dark and blundering growth. It is an attempt to approximate man to the method of vegetable and animal existence. The earth is a world of Life and Matter, but man is neither a vegetable nor an animal; he is a spiritual and a thoughtful being who is set here to shape and use the animal mould for higher purposes, by higher motives, with a more divine instrumentation.

In the historic ages of the present cycle of civilisation the movement has been almost entirely centred in the twin continents of Asia and Europe. And there it has been often seen that when Asia was moving through the light, Europe was passing through one of her epochs of obscurity and on the other hand the nights of Asia's repose or stagnation have corresponded with the days of Europe's mental vigour and vital activity.

But the fundamental difference has been that Asia has served predominantly (not exclusively) as a field for man's spiritual experience and progression; Europe has been rather a workshop for his mental and vital activities. As the cycle progressed, the Eastern continent has more and more converted itself into a store-house of spiritual energy sometimes active and reaching forward to new development, sometimes conservative and quiescent. Three or four times in history a stream of this energy has poured out upon Europe, but each time Europe has rejected wholly or partially the spiritual substance of the afflatus and used it rather as an impulse to fresh intellectual and material activity and progress. The first attempt was the filtering of Egyptian, Chaldean and Indian wisdom through the thought of the Greek philosophers from Pythagoras to Plato and the Neo-Platonists; the result was the brilliantly intellectual and unspiritual civilisation of Greece and Rome. But it prepared the way for the second attempt when Buddhism and Vaishnavism, filtered through the Semitic temperament, entered Europe in the form of Christianity. Christianity came within an ace of spiritualising and even of asceticising the mind of Europe; it was baffled by its own theological deformation in the minds of the Greek fathers of the Church and by the sudden flooding of Europe with a German barbarism whose temperament in its merits no less than in its defects was the very anti-type, both of the Christian spirit and the Graeco-Roman intellect.

The Islamic invasion of Spain and the southern coast of the Mediterranean—curious as the sole noteworthy example of Asiatic culture using the European method of material and political irruption as opposed to a peaceful invasion by ideas—may be regarded as a third attempt. The result of its meeting with Graecised Christianity was the reawakening of the European mind in feudal and Catholic Europe and the obscure beginnings of modern thought and science.

The fourth and last attempt which is as yet only in its slow initial stage is the quiet entry of Eastern and chiefly of Indian thought into Europe first through the veil of German metaphysics, more latterly by its subtle influence in reawakening the Celtic, Scandinavian and Slavonic idealism, mysticism, religionism, and the direct and open penetration of Buddhism, Theosophy, Vedantism, Bahaism and other Oriental influences in both Europe and America. On the other hand, there have been two reactions of Europe upon Asia; first the invasion of Alexander with his aggressive Hellenism which for a time held Western Asia, created echoes and reactions in India and returned through Islamic culture upon medieval Europe; secondly, the modern onslaught of commercial, political, scientific Europe upon the moral, artistic and spiritual cultures of the East.

Intellectual and materialistic Europe found India, the Asia of Asia, the heart of the world's spiritual life, in the last throes of an enormous experiment, the thought of a whole nation concentrated for centuries upon the pure spiritual existence to the exclusion of all real progress in the practical and mental life of the race. The entering stream of Eastern thought found in Europe the beginning of an era which rejected religion, philosophy and psychology—religion as an emotional delusion, philosophy, the pure essence of the mind, as a barren thought-weaving, and resolved to devote the whole intellectual faculty of man to a study of the laws of material nature and of man's bodily, social, economic and political existence and to build there on a superior civilisation.

That stupendous effort is over; it as not yet frankly declared its bankruptcy, but it is bankrupt. It is sinking in a cataclysm as gigantic and as unnatural as the attempt which gave it birth. On the other hand, the exaggerated spirituality of the Indian effort has also registered a bankruptcy; we have seen how high individuals can rise by it, but we have seen also how low a race can fall which in its eagerness to seek after God ignores. His intention in humanity. Both the European and the Indian attempt were admirable, the Indian by its absolute spiritual sincerity, the European by its severe intellectual honesty and ardour for the truth; both have accomplished miracles; but in the end God and Nature have been too strong for the Titanism of the human spirit and for the Titanism of the human intellect. The salvation of the human race lies in a more sane and integral development of the possibilities of mankind in the individual and in the community. It is not any exchange of forms that is required, but an interchange of regenerating impulses and a happy fusion and harmonising.

The synchronism and mutual interpenetration of the two great currents of human effort at such a crisis in the history of the race is full of hope for the future of humanity, but full also of possible dangers. The hope is the emergence of a new and better human life founded on a greater knowledge, a pursuit of the new faculties and possibilities opening out before us and a just view of the problem which the individual, the society, the race have to solve. Mankind has been drawn together by the developments of material science and for good or evil its external future is henceforth one; its different parts no longer develop separately and in independence of each other. There opens out at the same time the possibility that by the development and practice of the science and the life of the soul it may be made one in reality and by an internal unity.

The idea by which the enlightenment of Europe has been governed is the passion for the discovery of the Truth and Law that constitutes existence and governs the process of the world, the attempt to develop the life and potentialities of man, his ideals, institutions, organisation by the knowledge of that Law and Truth and the confidence that along this line lies the road of human progress and perfection. The idea is absolutely just and we accept it entirely; but its application has been erroneous. For the Law and Truth that has to be discovered is not that of the material world—though this is required, nor even of the mental and physical—though this is indispensable, but the Law and Truth of the Spirit on which all the rest depends. For it is the power of the Self of things that expresses itself in their forms and processes.

The message of the East to the West is a true message, "Only by finding himself can man be saved", and "What shall it profit a man though he gain the whole world, if he lose his own soul". The West has heard the message and is seeking out the law and truth of the soul and the evidence of an inner reality greater than the material. The danger is that with his passion for mechanism and his exaggerated intellectuality she may fog herself in an external and false psychism, such as we see arising in England and America, the homes of the mechanical genius, or in intellectual, unspiritual and therefore erroneous theories of the Absolute, such as have run their course in critical and metaphysical Germany.

The message that the West brings to the East is a true message. Man also is God and it is through his developing manhood that he approaches the godhead; Life also is the Divine, its progressive expansion is the self-expression of the Brahman, and to deny Life is to diminish the Godhead within us. This is the truth that returns to the East from the West translated into the language of the higher truth the East already possesses; and it is an ancient knowledge. The East also is awaking to the message. The danger is that Asia may accept it in the European form, forget for a time her own law and nature and either copy blindly the West or make a disastrous amalgam of that which she has in its most inferior forms and the crudenesses which are invading her.

The effort involves a quest for the Truth that underlies existence and the fundamental Law of its self-expression in the universe—the work of metaphysical philosophy and religious thought; the sounding and harmonising of the psychological methods of discipline by which man purifies and perfects himself—the work of psychology, not as it is understood in Europe, but the deeper practical psychology called in India Yoga and the application of our ideas to the problems of man's social and collective life. What then shall be our ideal? Unity for the human race by an inner oneness and not only by an external association of interests; the resurgence of man out of the merely animal and economic life or the merely intellectual and aesthetic into the glories of the spiritual existence; the pouring of the power of the spirit into the physical mould and mental instrument so that man may develop his manhood into that true supermanhood which shall exceed our present state as much as this exceeds the animal state from which Science tells us that we have issued. These three are one; for man's unity and man's self-transcendence can come only by living in the Spirit.

Elements, Mission and Aspiration of Indian Society

6

'An Enduring Tradition', the title of the Introductory Chapter of *Historic India*, a Life-Time publication, authored by Lucille Schulberg, begins with the significant passage, Historic India is not a country. It is a culture, one of the oldest and the most consistent on earth. That culture has been contemporary to almost all civilizations. It existed in nascent form, when the sun rose on Egypt's first kingdom in the fourth millennium B.C. Well developed, it was present when the sun sparkled on classical Greece in the fifth century B.C., and set on the British Empire in this (twentieth) century. This sums up the nature of Indian society in which political life was subjugated under the wider profound cultural life which has endured since the beginning of human civilization and is poised for a promising future. In the words of Sri Aurobindo, 'This nation is not a new race raw from the workshop of Nature or created by modern circumstances. One of the oldest races and greatest civilizations on this earth, the most indomitable in vitality, the most fecund in greatness, the deepest in life, the most wonderful in potentiality, after taking into itself numerous sources of strength from foreign strains of blood and other types of human civilization, is now seeking to lift itself for good into an organized national unity'.

In the evolutionary history of mankind society precedes the state. A society, a great human collectivity is an organic being with a common soul, mind and body. The life of the society passes through a cycle of birth, growth, youth, ripeness, decline, decadence and may perish or possesses the inherent capacity to renew itself, recover and start a new cycle. All the older peoples and nations except India and China have perished. Each communal soul is a manifestation and vehicle of the greater eternal spirit that expresses itself in Time and is seeking its own fullness in humanity through the vicissitudes of the human cycles. "A people", says Mahayogi Sri Aurobindo, "which learn to live consciously not solely in its physical and outward life, not even only in that and in the power of the life idea or soul idea that governs the changes of its development and is the key to its psychology and its temperament, but in the soul and the spirit behind may not at all exhaust itself, may not end by disappearance or a dissolution or a fusion into others or have to give place to new race or people, but having itself fused into its life many original societies and attained to its maximum natural growth pass without death through many renaissances. And even if at any time it appears to be on the point of absolute exhaustion and dissolution, it may recover by the force of the spirit and begin another and perhaps a more glorious cycle. The history of India has been that of the life of such people". India is on the verge of heralding such a glorious cycle.

NATURE OF INDIAN SOCIETY

The Epitome of Human Culture

The Indian Society is characterised by unity in diversity. In its social system there was place for every man. It has been hospitable to numerous groups of immigrants coming from different parts of Asia and Europe which have received unasked natural freedom of Indian culture to maintain their separate identity and way of life with dignity and equality. The Jews left their home after the advent of Christianity and dispersed to other places in the globe. One group came to India and found a honoured place compared to their other brethren who went elsewhere. Syrian Christians came during the early years of Christianity and were welcome. Parsis left Iran to protect their religion and culture and found a safe place. Though small in number, they occupy a position of prestige and pride. Muslims also came to India and settled long before Islam came in waves of force and aggression. All races and cultures have come and found a place here. India, thus, is not only an epitome of the world geographically but also an epitome of human cultures.

The Geographical Determinants

The present Indian landmass didn't exist millions of years ago before Mid-Eocene, 50 million years ago. The landmass south of the *Aravali Mountain* was a part of *Gondwana Land* which was connected with Mauritious in the West and the South-East-Asian archipelago in the East. *The Sea of Tethys* separated *Gondwana* from Eurasian Landmass. The geological upheaval due to the movement of these two landmasses towards each other led to the elevation of the *Himalayas* in three successive phases during the Tertiary Period: in Mid-Eocene, Mid-Miocene and Post-Pliocene respectively. The last continued upto latter half of Pleistocene. The waters of *the Sea of Tethys split* over to become the Bay of Bengal and the Arabian Sea. After the breaking up of the Gondwana land, the Peninsula of India began to acquire its present characteristic triangular shape.

The Himalayas, containing the highest mountain peaks of the globe, are in fact, among the youngest mountain chains of the world and occupy bio-geographically a predominant position being the Radiating Centre of World's three Great Bio-geographical Regions, namely the Indo-Malayan (the richest in the world), the Eurasian and the Afra-tropical. In the words of India's Classical Poet Kalidasa, "The King of Mountains, named *Himalaya* (the Abode of Snow), the Soul of Gods, washed by the Seas on the East and the West, stands on the North like a Balancing Rod of the Earth". Thus was formed, India of today, endowed with the widest variety of biomas, served by a wide network of fourteen River Valley Systems, the Himalayas providing immense fertility and comparative seclusion from the rest of the world, the geographical factors which shaped the evolution of India's culture.

The Racial Elements

To understand human race, we will have to know the rise and the divergent evolution of man, where and when man arose?

Science, Man and the Concept of Race

Based on the study of radioactive minerals in the earth's crust and radiocarbon dating the following events have been ascertained:

4.5 billion years ago	: the earth was born
3.5 billion years ago	: the first living things appeared on this planet
70 million years ago	: the first primates evolved
3 million years ago	: the earliest hominids, the forerunners of man appeared
700,000 to 250,000 years	: *Homo sapiens*, the human species, ago evolved.
50,000 years ago	: *Homo sapiens*, to which all human beings belong to today appeared

The first animals to which the name man is definitely assigned were the Java man (*Homo erectus*) and the Peking man (*Homo erectus pekinensis*). The distribution of *Homo erectus* was most probably not confined to China and eastern Asia. Probably it extended to Europe and even may be to Africa. As *Homo erectus* spread, it differentiated into many races. Out of one of these races evolved *Homo sapiens*. Which one? Where? *Homo sapiens* also increased in number and spread to new countries and differentiated into different races like Rhodesian man (*Homo sapiens rhodesiansis*) found in South Africa and Rhodesia, Soloman (*Homo sapiens soloensis*) found in Java and Neanderthal man (*Homo sapiens neanderthalensis*) found throughout Europe, western and central Asia. Cro-Magnon man or for that matter modern man (*Homo sapiens*) has derived its genetic equipment from all the different gene pools of different races that were made available. So mankind is both polytypic and polymorphic and the evolutionary history of man was anagenetic (straight) and not cladogenetic (branching). All human beings living on this earth today came from a common stock, *Homo sapiens*. Each human being carries from 20,000 to 100,000 different genes; each of these genes has one or more alleles or alternative expression(s). Around one third of human genes have two or more alleles.

Thus human genotypes are enormously complicated, but the physical or phenotypic differences exhibited by humans involve only a small number of genes and alleles and are relatively superficial. *The great diversity seen in the human species today is the result of its global distribution, geographical separation and reproductive isolation*, a process of divergent evolution. Either they replaced the regional archaic populations or interbred with them are subjects of debate. A geographically separated and reproductively isolated population possesses a common biological ancestry and an ensemble of unique, genetically transmitted traits and characteristics which distinguishes it from other populations.

Among *Homo sapiens* there were several subspecies but only one of those is extant today, namely, *Homo sapiens*. The subspecies, *Homo sapiens*, to which all human beings throughout the world belong to appeared around 50,000 years ago. From that time on it has not changed physically in any significant way. Therefore, the entire world human population belongs to one race, the human race. So the term race should be used to the entire extant human beings; it is scientifically incorrect to refer to the many varieties of *Homo sapiens* as races or subspecies. They may be conideed as ethnic groups. Georges Buffon (1749) in his Natural History generally described several population groups as races. Since then, on the basis of different criteria, varieties of mankind have been classified differently as human 'races' during last two and half centuries in social and anthropological studies. See Tables below. *The 'races' should be considered as ethnic groups.*

ETHNIC CLASSIFICATION AND GROUPS ON DIFFERENT CRITERIA

Table 6.1: Different races (*Ethnic* Groups) Based on Different Criteria

Five 'Races'	Three 'Races'	Geographical 'Races'
Caucasian (White)	Caucasoid (White)	European
Mongolian (Yellow)	Mongoloid (Yellow)	African
Ethiopian (Black)	Negroid (Black)	Asiatic
American Indian (Red)		Indian
Malayan (Brown)		Australian
		Melanesian
		Polynesian
		Amerindian

Table 6.2: Racial (*Ethnic*) Characteristics of Modern Man

Primary Race			*Composite Races*	
Primary Race	*Primary Sub-Races*	*Composite Sub-Races*	*Composite Races*	*Secondary Races*
Negroid	1. African Negro 2. Nilitic Negro 3. Negrito		Melanesian-Papuan (Oceanic Negroid)	1. Melanesian 2. Papuan
Caucasoid (White, Eur-African, European)	1. Mediteranean 2. Ainu 3. Keltic 4. Nordic 5. Alpine 6. East Baltic	7. Armenoid 8. Dinaric *Residual Mixed Types* 9. Nordic Alpine 10. Nordic-Mediteranean	1. Australian (Archaic White + Tasmanian + Melanian-papuan) 2. Indo-Dravadian (Predominantly white: Classic Medeterranean + Aus traloid + Negrito + minor fractions of Iranian or Armenoid, Nordic, Mongoloid) Morphological Types: - Classical Dravidian - Armenoid - Iranian - Indo-Nordic - Australoid (Veddoid) - Negritoid 3. Polynesian	
Mongoloid	1. Classic Mongoloid 2. Arctic Mongoloid (Eskimoid)		1. Indonesian-Mongoloid (Indonesian-Malay) (Mongoloid + Mediteranian + Ainu + Negrito) 2. American Indian (Mongoloid + Iranian + Australoid + Negritoid)	1. Malay-Mongol 2. Indonesian

(*Note*: Migrations and intermingling in the passage of time have resulted in Primary Races, Primary Sub-Race, Composite Sub-Races within the different stocks of Primary Races, Composite Races and Secondary Races)

According to Earnest Albert Hooton, Professor of Anthropology, Harvard University, "The hundreds of millions who inhabit India are not physically homogeneous, yet various ethnic strains have fused to create a distinctive composite race that is of predominantly White Origin. For this race the name Indo-Dravidian is employed here instead of the former term Dravidian. 'Dravidian' is a linguistic name, properly applicable to many of the darker and more primitive people of the southern part of the Indian peninsula. The prefix 'Indo' is meant to signify that the composite race also includes the civilised people that speak Indo-Aryan languages, together with the Munda-speaking people. The various racial types that have contributed to the Indo-Dravidian blend have long been recognised by anthropologists, but...a survey and analysis of some fifty-one 'racial groups' by Dr. B.S. Guha has put the entire subject of the racial composition of India upon a firmer foundation".

Table 6.3: An Alternative Human Racial (*Ethnic*) Classification

Capoid	Congoid	Caucasoid	Australoid	Mongoloid
A. Khoid	A. Central African	A. Mediteranid • West Mediterranean • East Mediterranean • Dinaricized • South • Arabid	A. Veddoid • Remnant Australoid population in central and southern India	A. Northeast Asian
B. Sanid	B. Bambutid	B. Dinaric	B. Negritos	B. Southeast Asian
	C. Aethiopid	C. Alpine.	C. Melanesian	C. Micronesian Polynesian
		D. Ladogan	D. Australian-Tasmanian	D. Ainuid
		E. Nordish		E. Tungid
		F. Armenid		F. Amerindian
		G. Turanid		
		H. Irano Afgan		
		I. Indic or Nordindid		
		J. Dravidic		

Indian People: The Indo-Dravidian Composite Ethnic Group

Anthropologically, the Indian people as a whole may be considered as a predominantly white composite race called Indo-Dravidian. The basic racial elements which entered into the composition of Indian people, the Indo-Dravidian race, comprise of: Classic Mediterranean + Australoid (Vedoid) + Negrito + minor fractions of Iranian Plateau or Armenoid, Nordic, Mongoloid:

Classic Indo-Dravidian, an adulterated Mediterranean type: A long headed, short statured, classes of north India, to some extent, Punjab.

Australoid-Veddoid: A short-statured, curly-haired, chocolate-skinned type of dolichocephal, with prominent brow-ridges, depressed nasal root, broad nose, and prognathism; in central and southern India.

Negritoid: A submerged pygmoid strain with wooly hair and generally Negritoid features, in remote hill areas of south India and Andaman.

Armenoid-Iranian Plateau: A brunet, brachycephalic type with flattened occiput, convex nose, and heavy beard and body hair, in the western littoral and Bengal.

Indo-Nordic: A mixed Nordic type in the north-western Himalayan areas.

Mongoloids: Intrusive Mongoloid types along the Himalayan boarder and in north-eastern fringe.

Where did *Homo sapiens* and the main ethnic groups arise from? The evolution of Pongids and Hominids took place during Mid-Miocene to recent periods in Geological Time Scale. It is a remarkable coincidence that the second phase of evolution of the Himalayas also took place during Mid-Miocene. It is the *tri-junction and the radiating points of world's three great biomas*. Did the Himalayas play a major role in this evolutionary phase? Shiwalik fossil beds in the foothills of the Himalayas are rich in dryopithecine apes, i.e. *Dryopithecus*, *Bramapithecus*, *Ramapithecus*, *Sivapithecus*, *Sugrivapithecus*, who played a major role in ape evolution. But no Hominid fossil has been found yet anywhere in India. Evidence on Palaeolithic period and even of Neolithic period in India are still very meager. Though numerous Palaeolithic implements have been found in India, but no skeletal remains of Palaeolithic man or no skulls can safely be attributed to the Neolithic period. It is imperative to undertake intensive study in this direction to establish any opinion on a firm basis. There are various opinions about the original home of the Aryans.

Table 6.4: Original Home of Aryans

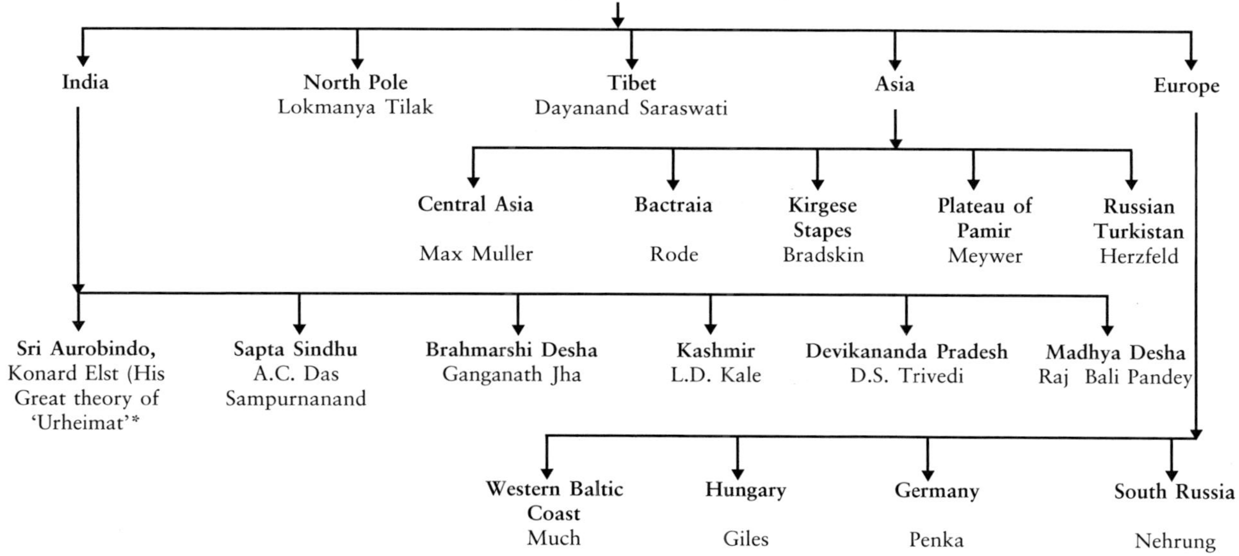

Source: *Guttor Francoic (1996) : *Rewriting Indian History*, Vikas Publication House, New Delhi.

1. Mittal, A.K. (1994) : *Political and Cultural History of India*, Satya Bhawan, Agra.

The UNESCO Statements on Race

Two international symposia of scientists were sponsored by UNESCO following World War II and the Holocaust on the question of race. The outcome was two statements on race: the first by the social scientists and the second by the physical anthropologists and geneticists:

- *The first statement by social scientists (which included world renowned scholars like E. Franklin Frazier, Claude Levi-Strauss and Ashley Montagu) was published on July 18, 1950:* The likenesses among men are far greater than their differences. It would be better when speaking of the human races to drop the term 'race' altogether and speak of ethnic groups. The scientific material available to us at present does not justify the conclusion that inherited genetic differences are a major factor in producing differences between cultures and the cultural experience which each group has undergone is the major factor in explaining such differences.

  The one trait which above all others has been at a premium in the evolution of man's mental character has been educability, plasticity. This is a trait that all human beings possess. There is no biological justification for prohibiting inter-marriage between persons of different ethnic groups. For all practical social purposes 'race' is not so much a biological phenomenon as a social myth. The range of mental capacities of all ethnic groups is much the same.
- *The second statement by physical anthropologists and geneticists (which included distinguished personalities like J.B.S. Haldane, Thomas Dobzhansky and Julian Huxley) was issued on July 15, 1952:* All men living today belong to a single species, Homo Sapiens, and are derived from a common stock. The differences in physical structure which distinguish one major group from another give no support to the popular notions of any general 'superiority' or 'inferiority' which are sometimes implied in referring to these groups. There is

no evidence for the existence of so-called 'pure' races. Genetic differences are of little significance in determining the social and cultural differences between different groups of men.

The Language Elements

The languages of Indian people can be traced to four speech-families:

- the Austric otherwise called the Kol or Munda, mostly confined to the hill tribes,
- the Tibeto-Chinese or Sino-Tibetian, confined to the eastern fringe,
- the Dravidian, and
- the Aryan or the Indo-European.

The texture of most of the modern Indian Languages has been produced by the combination of the speech of the Early Dravidians and that of the Vedic Aryans the former predominating in the region south of the river Godavari. Sri Aurobindo found, "On examining the vocabulary of the Tamil language, in appearance so foreign to the Sanskrit form and character, I yet found myself continuously guided by words, or families of words supposed to be pure Tamil, in establishing new relations between Sanskrit and its distant sister, Latin, and occasionally between the Greek and the Sanskrit. Sometimes the Tamil vocabulary not only suggested the connection but proved the missing link in a family of connected words. And it was through the Dravidian language that I came first to perceive what seems to me now the true law, origin and, as it were, the embryology of the Aryan tongues. The possibility suggests itself that they may even have been two diversions, or families derived from one lost primitive tongue".

The latest finding at Mehargarh indicates that the Indus Valley Civilisation is one of the oldest and is contemporary to Egyptian and Sumerian Civilisations. Who built this and when? There is great controversy.

The Elements of Castes

The dominant nature of Indian society which is obvious and a paradox to any one is the institution of caste. Each caste stands for a way of life, governed by its own rules and regulations and customs. These are most obvious especially in matters of marriage, food and various rituals, the persistence of the racial memory linked to *kula parampara* (family/clan tradition) and *jati parampara* (caste tradition) which have occupied honoured, dignified, independent and equal place in the organisation of wider cultural life of the entire Indian society. This metaphysical democracy is the dominant nature of *Indian psyche* and its culture. The sense of democracy, freedom and equality is native to the Indian mind and flows in its vein and not superfluous and determined by externalities. Caste system, rather *jati* system is prevalent in India, as stated earlier, not only in the predominant Hindu population, but also among Muslims and Christians.

Hindus

Hindu population is organised into castes. People are born into one of several thousand caste groups. The peoples' lives are greatly influenced and determined by the castes to which they are born.

- Families belonging to a caste generally perform work handed over from generation to generation. In rural society, generally, some vocation like farming may be open to everyone. But generally the castes are recognised by the type of work their members do (barber, iron-smith, goldsmith, carpenter, leather worker, potter, washer-man, priests, etc.).
- People marry within the same caste (endogamous).
- People generally believe that their life's desires and aspirations will be fulfilled through performing their duties sincerely which have been provided to them automatically.
- People feel pride in their caste and trace their ancestry to a saint or rishi born in the past and try to emulate the values for which he attained fame.

- There are thousands of castes but are divided into four main orders: *brahmins, kshatriya, vaishya* and *shudra.*
- People believe that their birth into a caste is no bar to rise to any height in the realisation of four *purusharthas: dharma, artha, kama* and *moksha.*
- People also believe that any individual from any caste, from the lowest of the low to the highest of the high, can free himself or herself from the rigidity of the social caste system by becoming a *sanyasi* or *sanyasini,* and get respect from all.
- Caste system, so far as jobs and social position are concerned, has lost their meaning due to changing times:
  - Transportation and mobility.
  - Newer economical opportunities of classes.
  - Opening of facilities to acquire new skills.
  - Migration to urban areas in search of new pastures.

Muslims

Among the Indian Muslims, the distinction between the Ashrafs, the 'honourable' and the Ailafs other Muslims, in U.P. can be compared with the prevalence of distinction between the 'twice-born' and other Hindus. The Ashrafs are considered as descendants of foreign, non-Indian ancestors and are traditionally the land-owners, the religious and civic leaders and the wealthiers. Four classes of Ashrafs are found in UP—the Sayyads, the Sheikhs, the Mughals and the Pathans. The Sayyad line is descended from the daughter of the prophet and her husband, the fourth Caliph of Islam.

There are around twenty sections among the Sayyads. Endogamy is common within each section but is not mandatory. The Sheikhs are considered to be descended from Arab ancestors. Marriages are contracted within their sections and Sayyads but rarely with the families of the Mughals and Pathans. The Mughals and the Pathans are considered to be the descendents of the Mongols and Afghans. No member of an Ashraf group will marry a non-Ashraf or even take food. Next rank among

Muslims is constituted by the Muslims of the 'clean occupational castes' whose ancestors were Hindu Rajputs who were converted to become Muslims.

The lowest among the Muslims are the ones who do scavanging, sweeping and other menial jobs. They have descended from the converts who retained their former caste name, occupation, and disabilities. The higher ranked Muslims do not ordinarily take food from them. In villages they are not allowed to enter and pray inside the village mosque but stand outside and pray. There is gradually a broader acceptability of inter-dining especially in urban areas. Social changes are evident among Muslims as among Hindus.

New castes have arisen from indigenous Muslims as they have arisen in Hindu sects. Two major sects of Islam, Sunni and Shia, came to India with Islam. Both have been further divided in India. One offshoot of the Shia is that of Ismaili, some of whom regard the Aga Khan as their head. The Bohras and Khojas of Gujarat are two other major groups of Ismaili. A Syrian of Jewish origin founded a Muslim cult which included Jewish, Christian and Hindu rites. Several Muslim sects gave honour to Hindu deities.The Ahmadiyas is a modern section of Muslims founded in the late nineteenth century. It is a combination of modem enterprise and fundamentalist theology.

Jews, Christians and *Parsis* have been in India since more than a millennium and settled in local Indian social systems as separate *jati* members.

Jews

The oldest settlements of Jews were in Cochin in Kerala and also in Maharashtra.There were two groups of Jews, White and Black. The White Jews would not inter-marry or inter-line with the Black Jews. A third *jati* evolved from the converts of the servants of the White Jews.

Christians

Indian Christians can be distinguished into two distinct categories, ancient and modern. The *ancient Christians* are popularly known as *Syrian Christians*, who came to India long back more than a millennium years ago and settled along Kerala coast, made some converts and established permanent Christian Groups in Kerala. The *modern Christians* evolved when the European missionaries came in sixteenth century along with colonisers and seized political controls. These Missionaries were professionally dedicated to convert local people. Their work was supported by the European Christian rulers who seized political powers. The equalities of status among Christian societies was confined to the hours of Church worship. Change of religion for the converts changed little their ritual and social characteristics inherited from their Hindu caste traditions and norms.

Parsis

Parsis came to India in about the eighth century. They live as one community in Indian social system. Culturally and financially they occupy a prestigious position in India.

The Disinformation on Indian Heritage

Francois Gautier, in his recent publication (1996), *Rewriting Indian History*, has demolished three erroneous views of the Western Historians on Indian History and heritage followed blindly by historians throughout the world including most Indian historians without ascertaining truth and prevalent in history textbooks world over not excluding India. He has discussed his views in the Chapter on "The Tainted Glass: A look at Western Civilization" under three disinformations on India.

- The First Disinformation on India: Aryans vs Dravidians
- The Second Disinformation: The Vedas
- The Third Disinformation: The Caste System.

The First Disinformation on India: Aryans vs Dravidians

Many pre-Christian sects in Palestine were under the influence of Hinduism and Buddhism. The legends surrounding the birth of Christ are similar to that of Krishna and Buddha. Most probably Christ came to India for spiritual initiation. The structure of the church resembles those of the Buddhist Chaitya.

The early asceticism of the early Christians might have been influenced by Jainism.

Christianity influenced the Western world greatly when barbarism was the order of the day for many countries. It brought sanity in a world of rape, black plague, murder and chaos. Thus, the Western civilization is being intimately associated with Christianity though it has taken many forms. During the era of colonialism, the colonial powers encouraged the Christian missionaries to convert the conquered people to their brand of religion with the full assistance of the military authority of their armies. With their commitment and sincerity to their faith and bringing the virtues of Western civilization-medicine, education and salvation–to the conquered people who were considered by them as nothing but savages, barbarians and pagans, wherever 'the Soldiers of Christ' went, they exterminated centuries old ways of life and culture and replaced them with their totally inadequate system altering civilizations radically and changing pattern of thinking. After three generations the children of the conquered had forgotten their roots and looked upon the conquered as their benefactors. That is how, the entire civilization of the Incas and the Aztecs, one of the most magnificent ever, was annihilated in South America by the Spanish soldiers and the Priests.

India was already familiar with Christianity since the arrival of the Syrian Christians in first century A.D. who had become part and parcel of Indian life in Kerala. But the Christian Missionaries who came with the colonial powers discovered that Hinduism accepted all religions as true and included in its fold even creeds contrary to its main stream philosophy. They found the average man here adored his motherland. The people were blended together as an organic whole. A supreme sense of self-respect, freedom, devotion to their culture were ingrained in their blood. They found it difficult to convert. The endurance and sincere attachment to their own faith led the missionaries to go into the roots of the vitality and strength of Hinduism in India.

These roots nourish the Hindu Society. Unless these are destroyed or dried up no proslitizing religion can find success.

"Thus was born", writes Francois Gautier, "the great Aryan invasion theory, of two civilizations, that of the low caste Dravidians and the high caste Brahmins and Kshatriyas, always pitted against each other, which has endured till today and has been used by all Western historians and unfortunately by most Indian textbooks too. Sound preposterous? Simplistic? Impossible? Yet this theory not only helped the missionaries to play the Untouchables against the hated Brahmins who, let it be said, managed single handedly to preserve orally Hindu culture and religion for five millennia. It also suited the British, who found it an ideal channel to push forward their divide and rule policies." Macaulay, the brain behind the system of English education, wrote in 1836 to his father, "No Hindu who has received English education ever remains sincerely attached to his religion". Neither archaeological evidence nor trace anywhere of a struggle between the Dravidians and the Aryans have been found.

The battle between Rama and Ravana is cited as instance of the above struggle. But ask a child anywhere in India from North or South the answer you get is Ravana is the son of a Brahmin. How come fight between two races? The Dutch sociologist Konard Elst holds the view of indigenous Indians. He supports his views with the recent accumulation of evidence which indicates that Vedic culture and Harappan (Dravidian) culture are one and the same and propounds his great theory of *"Urheimat"*:

- Aryans were originally in India.
- Aryans migrated from India outwards to Iran, then to Turkestan, and then to Europe.

The Second Disinformation: The Vedas

The disinformation about the Vedas as 'the root of all evil' and 'the source of paganism' was started with the missionaries who went on belittling it as a set of pagan offerings. This view was perpetuated by most Western historians. They saw in the Vedas little of spiritual values and post-dated them to 1500-1000 B.C. which have been followed blindly by not only historians throughout the world through the medium of modern civilization ushered by the West but ridiculously by most Indian historians without ascertaining the truth.

Mr. Gautier argues, "Why did historians show such an eagerness to post-dating the Vedas and making of them just mumble-jumble of pagan superstition? Because it would have destroyed the West's idea of its own supremacy. Primitive barbarism could not possibly have risen to such high conceptions so early particularly when the Westerners have started our era after the birth of Christ and decreed that the world began on 23rd October 4000 B.C." Recent researches including Carbon-14 analysis at Mehergarh and other sites in the Indus Valley have shown that the Indus Civilization had its beginning between 7000 and 6000 B.C. Though the last of the great civilizations to be discovered and a late comer in history books, the Indus civilization is the oldest of the great civilizations.

In this context one instance, historically significant, can be cited. A canister containing a valuable manuscript was found deep down in the earth when the Chinese Wall was blown off during the bombing operation by the Japanese in 1932. The manuscript gives a peep into the ancient civilization of China. The author had given a brief history of the manuscript, the circumstances under which he wrote it. The Emperor Chin Ize Wang, to perpetuate himself as the greatest patron of learning and wisdom which took birth only during his reign, had all the historical records describing the ancient glory of China burnt. The author of the manuscript restored the history of China and in a preparatory note stated the reason of his burying his manuscript so deeply into the earth. This manuscript was bought by Sir Augustus Fritz George who brought to London and handed it over to a group of Chinese experts headed by Professor Anthony Graeme. The latter showed it to Sir Wallace Budge of the British Museum who remarked that the manuscript was of even greater value than the Codex Siaiticus. In the manuscript they found direct reference to the Laws of Manu, which were first written in the Vedic language 10,000 years ago. The reference was found about a distinct relationship between the people of India, America and China as well as about the ruined cities which have been found in the centre of Peruvian forests.

What happened to this manuscript, one of the greatest findings of human history? Can it be traced in the British Museum since it was moved out of its premises during the war and no manuscript was shipped to the USA for safety? What about the Vedas? *'The compendium of primitive pagans' rituals?* as the Western scholars would term? Unfortunately for such scholars, very recently a congruence of Modern Science and Vedic Science is taking place through the effort of Maharishi Mahesh Yogi. A student of Physics himself, when he came to know from major scientists of the recent advances of Unified Field Theory in physics, he asserted, "The knowledge of the Unified Field has been discovered by modern science during just the last few years but the complete knowledge of the Unified Field has always been available in the Vedic literature" (1986). Prof. Kenneth Chandler writes, "Modern Experimental Science and Maharishi's Vedic Science could now be seen as two diverse yet mutually complementary approaches to knowing the same underlying reality—one through the empirical method, the other through the exploration of the least excited state of consciousness". The theme of exploring Modern Science and Vedic Science to discover structural similarities in their description of the Unified Field have attracted eminent unified field theorists, mathematicians and physiologists including a number of Nobel Laureates.

The Third Disinformation: The Caste System

The disinformation is propagated that it is the Aryans who imposed the caste system on the Dravidians and the primitive people. The Hindu society is exploited in the name of caste system by every body: in the last two centuries by the missionaries, Muslims, Hindu intellectuals of all denominations, secular historians and politicians; and after independence, by the Indian politicians, each to fulfil its own purpose. But what is the truth? Is it an imposition by the Aryans on the Dravidians or primitive people? What was the original purpose of caste system? Was it a natural division of people to serve a purpose in the society? Has it degenerated? Since when? All races and cultures throughout the world have people who are divisible into different classes; one can see huge class differences even in present day Europe; is India's caste system really worse? Can it be excluded or eliminated? One must not forget that castes not only exist among Hindus but also among Christians and Muslim in India. This is an Indian heritage. To understand it, we will have to go back to ancient India.

The Great Synthesis: Unity in Diversity

The psyche of Indian society has been shaped and nurtured for more than three millennia by two epics, *Ramayana* and *Mahabharata*. Both are considered as the *niti-shastra* and the *samaja-shastra*, the scriptures on ethics and sociology respectively. The First Indian Governor General of Independent India, Chakravarti Rajagopalachari, popularly known as Rajaji, in his preface to the second edition of his work, *Mahabharata*, a Bharatiya Vidya Bhavan publication, writes, "The *Mahabharata* discloses a rich civilisation and a highly evolved society which, though of an older world, strangely resembles the India of our own time, with the same values and ideals.....The caste system prevailed, but inter-caste marriages were not unknown. Some of the greatest warriors in the *Mahabharata* were Brahmins.... The *Mahabharata* has moulded the character and civilisation of one of the most numerous of the world's people... if a foreigner reads this book—translation and epitome though it is—and closes it with a feeling that he has read a good and elevating work, he may be confident that he has grasped the spirit of India and can understand her people—high and low, rich and poor".

Various racial elements that have entered into the composition of the Indian people can be known from these two monumental epics. A great synthesis of all ethnic elements have taken place during the era of *Ramayana* and *Mahabharata*. Vasudeva, the father of Sri Krishna, the central figure in *Mahabharata*, was the son of Shoora who was born of a Naga woman, Kunti, mother of Pandavas was also the daughter of Shoora. Veda Vyas, the author of *Mahabharata*, was the son of an *Arya Rishi*, Parasara by a fisher girl. The latter became the queen of the Aryan ruler Santanu, great-grandmother of the Pandavas and Kauravas. Bhuima married Hidamba, a Nishada woman. The epic describes several dynastic-histories of royal houses who were non-Aryans. Jarasandha and Shalva were non-Aryans. The *Rishis* who hailed from all the extant groups of people laid the cultural foundation of Indian society by ensuring Unity in Diversity. The period between the wars of Parashurama of *Ramayana* time and the dawn of the Magadhan supremacy around seventh century B.C. is the post-Vedic period which witnessed great social synthesis.

Social Organic System: The Vedic Symbolism

The social stratification is a universal phenomenon. It exists in every society existing in the world. But what was the nature of stratification in Ancient India? What was the basis on which this system was developed? In his work, *The Human Cycle*, Sri Aurobindo explains, "The Vedic institution of the fourfold order, *chaturvarna,* miscalled the system of the four castes, for caste is a conventional, *varna* a symbolic and typal institution. We are told that the institution of the four orders of society was the result of an economic evolution complicated by political causes. Very possibly, but the important point is that it was not so regarded and could not be so regarded by the men of that age. For a while we are satisfied when we have found the practical and material causes of a social phenomenon and do not care to look farther, they cared little or only subordinately for its material factors and looked always first and foremost for its symbolic, religious or psychological significance.

This appears in the Purushasukta of the *Veda* where the four orders are described as having sprung from the body of the creative Deity, from his head, arms, thighs and feet. To us, this is merely a poetical image and its sense is that the *Brahmins* were the men of knowledge, the *Kshatriyas* the men of power, the *Vaishyas* the producers and support of society, the *Shudra* its servants.... We read always our own mentality into that of these ancient forefathers and it is therefore that we can find in them nothing but imaginative barbarians. To us, poetry is a revel of intellect and fancy, imagination, a plaything and caterer for our amusement, our entertainer, the nautch-girl of the mind.

But to the men of old the poet was a seer, a revealer of hidden truths, imagination no dancing courtesan but a priestess in God's house commissioned not to spin fictions but to image difficult and hidden truths; even the metaphor or simile in the Vedic style is used with a serious purpose and expected to convey a reality, not to suggest a pleasing artifice of thought. The image was to these seers, a revelative symbol of the unrevealed and it was used because it could hint luminously to the mind what the precise intellectual word, *apt* only for logical or practical thought or to express the physical and the superficial, could not at all hope to manifest. To them this symbol of the Creator's body was more than an image, it expressed a divine reality.

Human society was for them, an attempt to express in life the cosmic Purusha who has expressed himself otherwise in the material and the supraphysical universe. Man and the cosmos are both symbols and expressions of the same hidden Reality. "From this symbolic attitude came the tendency to make everything in society a sacrament, religious and sacrosanct, but as yet with a large and vigorous freedom in all its forms".

Table 6.5: Social Organic System: The Vedic Symbolism

ORDER	*Cosmic Principle*	*Manifestation of Divine in Man*	*The body parts of creative Deity, Divine Purusha*	*Chaturvarnya, the social expression of Divine Purusha*	*Purushartha*
1	The Wisdom that conceives the order and principle of things	The Divine as Knowledge	Head	The man of Knowledge (*Brahmin*)	*Dharma, Artha, Kama, Moksha*
2	The Power that sanctions, upholds and enforces it	The Divine as Power	Arms	The man of power (*Kshatriya*)	*Dharma, Artha, Kama, Moksha*
3	The Harmony that creates the arrangement of the parts	The Divine as production, enjoyment and mutuality	Thigh	The producer and support of society (*Vaishya*)	*Dharma, Artha, Kama, Moksha*
4	The Work that carries out what they rest direct	The Divine as service, obedience and work	Feet	The man of service, the labour, (*Shudra*)	*Dharma, Artha, Kama, Moksha*

Formative and Vitalising Elements of Indian Culture

The formative and vitalising elements of Indian culture were provided by the Vedic culture. The basic social institutions of this culture were—the *Kula,* the family, the *Jana,* the tribe, the *Panchajana,* the federation of the tribes. The indissolubility of the *kula* was one of the fundamental values which was preserved by ceremonial offerings like *pritriyajna, tarpana, pindadana and shraddha* and made the ancestors, father and mother and sons and daughters one in spirit, tradition and property. The *kula* provided tradition and norms of conduct, trained members from infancy to collective action inspired by love sacrifice and pride of parentage. The *kula* thus became the perenial source of stability, continuity and vitality. The *kula* belongs to *a gotra* which takes its genesis from a *rishi* (seer). The marital bond was sublimated through marriage vows which fused two personalities into one. The norms and values and virtues of family life were kept with meticulous care for Gods, Goddesses, ancestors or *rishis* to take their birth to unite heaven and earth. So, the arrival of a child, boy or girl, was a event of great expectation and joy.

Yajna

It was the next important and effective socio-religious institution. *Yajna* is *sankalpita karma,* a promised work dedicated to the Divine. The sage says, '*yajno yajnena kalpatam*', the ritual *(yajna)* prospers when it is performed with the spirit of sacrifice *(yajna)*. The spirit is *tapa.* The strict observances of *yajna* manifested the power of *rita.* Any aspiration can be realised through sacrifice. With the sacrifice of Purusha, the Cosmic Being who pervaded the earth and transcended all directions, the Creation followed. The institution *(yajna)* brought men on earth and the Gods in heaven into close intimacy and linked together. It sowed the seeds of dedication and sacrifice in people to live for truth and well-being of one and all.

Rita

The Eternal Law, all-pervading, upholds Cosmic Order and is the source of strength of natural and spiritual power and beauty. Gods are Gods because they uphold it. *Rishis* (seers) are *Rishis* because they uphold it. That which does not conform to *Rita* is un-rita, untruth. *Rita* translated into conduct in accord with thought, word and deed becomes *Satya,* truth. *Rita* and *Satya* were born in the beginning of things out of *Tapa.*

Tapa

It is self-discipline for attaining purity of mind speech and body. It sublimates ego and urges and releases energy which sublimate human nature whose impact spreads and influences the family and social environment. *Tapa is yogashakti,* the consciousness force, the *chitshakti.* The world is upheld by *Rita, Satya, Tapa* and *Yajna* which are nourished by *Dharma.*

Dharma

In Indian culture is the foundation of life, next to spirit? What is *Dharma? Yatovyudayanihshreyasasiddhih sa dharmah:* that which enables and inspires human beings to evolve *(avyudaya)* and attain supreme fulfilment *(nihshreyasa)* is *Dharma. Dharanatdharmamityahuh dharmo dharayati praja: Dharma* arises out of the sustaining principle; it brings individuals together and sustain them as a society. The meanig *of Dharma* is two fold: it sustains and enables individuals to evolve in this world as well as inspires the aspirants to realise the life's goal; it is the power which binds individuals together and sustain them as a society. *Manusmriti* says, "the *Veda*, the consciousness force of the knower of the *Veda*, the conducts of the saints and the self-contentment are the roots of *Dharma*. The *Veda*, memory, good conduct and self-contentment are the four visible signs *of Dharma. Dharma* originates from *sadachara,* good conduct. Good conducts originated from India and practised by people of all *varnas* living in the sacred land of *Brahmavarta* located between the two rivers of *Saraswati* and *Drishadvati* and flow through tradition. All the people of the world would learn good conducts from the greatmen of this sacred land".

Dharma encompasses all ethical ideas. In the words of Sri Aurobindo, "There is no ethical idea which it has not stressed, put in its most ideal and imperative form, enforced by teaching, injunction, parable, artistic creation are formative examples. There are certain fundamental motives or essential ideal forces which cannot be thrown away, because they are part of the vital principles of our being and of the aim of Nature in us, our

Swadharma.... The right order of human life as of the universe is preserved, according to the ancient Indian idea, by each individual being following faithfully his *swadharma,* the true law and norm of his nature and the nature of his kind and by the group being, the organic collective life, doing likewise. The family, clan, caste, class, social, religious, industrial or other community, nation, people are all organic group beings that evolve their own *Dharma* and to follow it is the condition of their preservation, healthy continuity, sound action. There is also the *Dharma* of the position, the particular relation with others, as there is too the *Dharma* imposed by the condition, environment, age, *yugadharma,* the universal religious or ethical *Dharma,* and all these acting on the natural *Dharma,* the action according to the *swabhava,* create the body of Law.

The ancient theory supposed that in an entirely right and sound condition of man, individual and collective, a condition typified by the legendary Golden Age, *Satya Yuga*—Age of Truth—there is no need of any political Government or State or artificial construction of society, because all then live freely according to the truth of their enlightened self and God-inhabited being and therefore spontaneously according to the inner divine *Dharma*. The self-determining individual and self-determining community living according to the right and free law of his and its being is therefore the ideal. But in the actual condition of humanity, its ignorant and devious nature subject to perversions and violations of the true individual and the true social *Dharma*, there has to be super-imposed on the natural life of society, a State, a sovereign power, a king or governing body, whose business is not to interfere unduly with the life of the society, which must be allowed to function for the most part according to its natural law and custom and spontaneous development, but to superintend and assist its right process and see that the *Dharma* is observed and in vigour and, negatively, to punish and repress and, as far as may be, prevent offences against the *Dharma*.

Cultural Foundation of Indian Society (*Varnashrama Dharma*) in the Words of Sri Aurobindo

Indian culture from an early stage seized upon a double idea for its own guidance which it threw into a basic system of the individual life in the social frame. This was the double system of the four *Varnas* and the four *Ashramas,*—four graded classes of society and four successive stages of a developing human life. The ancient *Chaturvarnya* must not be judged by its latter disintegrated degeneration and gross meaningless parody, the caste system. But neither was it precisely the system of the classes which we find in other civilizations, priesthood, nobility, merchant class and serfs or labourers. It may have had outwardly the same starting point, but it was given a very different revealing significance. The ancient Indian idea was that man falls by his nature into four types. There are, first and highest, the man of learning and thought and knowledge; next, the man of power and action, ruler, warriors, administrator; third in the scale, the economic man, producer and wealth-getter, the merchant, artisan, cultivator; these were the twice-born, who received the initiation, *Brahmin, Kshatriya, Vaishya.* Last came, the more underdeveloped human type, not yet fit for these steps of the scale, unintellectual, without force, incapable of creation or intelligent production, the man fit only for unskilled labour and menial service, the *Shudra.*

The economic order of the society was cast in the form and gradation of these four types. The *Brahmin* class was called upon to give the community its priests, thinkers, men of letters, legislators, scholars, religious leaders and guides. The *Kshatriya* class gave it its kings, warriors, governors and administrators. The *Vaishya* order supplied it with its producers, agriculturists, craftsmen, artisans, merchants and traders. The *Shudra* class ministered to its need of menials and servants. As far as this went, there was nothing peculiar in the system except its extraordinary durability and perhaps, the supreme position given to religion, thought and learning, not at the top of the scale,—for that can be paralleled from one or other civilizations,—but as the dominant power.

The Indian idea in its purity fixed the status of a man in this order not by his birth, but by his capacities and his inner nature. It was a well-devised and necessary scheme in its time; it gave the community the firm and nobly built stability it needed for the security of its cultural development,—a stability hardly paralleled in any other culture. And as interpreted by the Indian genius, it became a greater thing than a mere outward economic, political and social mechanism intended to serve the needs and convenience of the collective life, for the real greatness of the Indian system of the four *Varnas* did not lie in its well-ordered division of economic function; its true originality and permanent value was in the ethical and spiritual content which the thinkers and builders of the society poured into these forms.

This inner content started with the idea that the intellectual, ethical and spiritual growth of the individual is the central need of the race. Society itself is only the necessary framework for this growth; it is a system of relations which provides it with its needed medium, field and conditions and with a nexus of helpful influences. A secure place had to be found in the community for the individual man from which he could at once serve these relations, helping to maintain the society and pay his debt of duty and assistance, and proceed to his own self-development with the best possible aid from the communal life. Birth was accepted in practice as the first gross and natural indicator; for heredity to the Indian mind has always ranked as a factor of the highest importance : it was even taken in later thought as a sign of the nature and as an index to the surroundings which the individual has prepared for himself by his past soul-development in former existences. But birth is not and cannot be the sole test of *Varna.*

The intellectual capacity of the man, the turn of his temperament, his ethical nature, his spiritual stature, these are the important factors. There erected therefore, a rule of family living, a system of individual observance and self-training, a force of upbringing and education which would bring out and formulate these essential things. The individual man was carefully trained in the practices, habits and attainments, and habituated to the sense of honour and duty necessary for the discharge of his allotted function in life. He was scrupulously equipped with the science of the thing he had to do, the best way to succeed in it as an interest, *artha,* and to attain to the highest rule, canon and recognised perfection of its activities—economic, political, sacerdotal, literary, scholastic or whatever else they might be.

Even the most despised pursuits had their education, their law and canon, their ambition of success, their sense of honour in the discharge and scruple of well-doing, their dignity of a fixed standard of perfection, and it was because they had these things that even the lowest and least attractive could be in a certain degree a means of self-finding and ordered self-satisfaction. In addition to this special function and training there were the general accomplishments, sciences, arts, graces of life, those which satisfy the intellectual, aesthetic and hedonistic powers of human nature. These in ancient India were many and various, were taught with minuteness, thoroughness and subtlety and was available to all men of culture.

But while there was provision for all these things and it was made with a vivid liberality of the life-spirit and a noble sense of order, the spirit of Indian culture did not, like other ancient culture, stop here. It said to the individual: "This is only the substructure: it is of a pressing importance indeed, but still not the last and greatest thing. When you have paid your debt to society, filled well and admirably your place in its life, helped its maintenance and continuity and taken from it your legitimate and desired satisfaction, there still remains the greatest thing of all. There is still your own self, the inner you, the soul which is a spiritual portion of the Infinite, one in its essence with the Eternal. This self, this soul in you, you have to find, you are here for that and it is from the place I have for you in life and by this training that you can begin to find it. For to each *Varna*, I have supplied its highest ideal of man-hood, the highest ideal way of which your nature is capable. By directing your life and nature in its own law of being towards that perfection, you cannot only grow towards the ideal and enter into harmony with universal nature but come also into nearness and contact with a greater nature of divinity and move towards transcendence.

That is the real object before you. From the life-basis I give you, you can rise to the liberating knowledge which brings spiritual release, *moksa*. Then you can grow out of all these limitations in which you are being trained; you can grow through the fulfilled *Dharma* and beyond it into the eternity of your self, into the fullness, freedom, greatness and bliss of the immortal spirit; for that is what each man is behind the veils of his nature. When you have done that you are free. Then you have gone beyond all the *Dharmas;* you are then a universal soul, one with all existence, and you can either act in that divine liberty for the good of all living things or else turn to enjoy in solitude the bliss of eternity and transcendence".

The whole system of society, founded on the four *Varnas,* was made a harmonious means for the elevation and progress of the soul, mind and life from the natural pursuit of interest and desire, first to the perfection of the law of our being, *Dharma,* and at the end to a highest spiritual freedom. For man's true end in life must be always this realisation of his own immortal self, this entry in its secret of an infinite and eternal existence.

The Indian system did not entirely leave this difficult growth to the individual's unaided inner initiative. It supplied him with a framework; it gave him a scale and gradation for his life which could be made into a kind of ladder rising in that sense. This high convenience was the object of the four *Ashramas.* Life was divided into four natural periods and each of them marked out a stage in the working out of this cultural idea of living. There was the period of the students, the period of the householder, the period of the recluse or forest-dweller, the period of the free super-social man, *parivrajaka.*

The student life was framed to lay the groundwork of what the man had to know, do and be. It gave a thorough training in the necessary arts, science, branches of knowledge, but it was still more insistent on the discipline of the ethical nature and in earlier days contained as as an indispensable factor a grounding in the Vedic formula of spiritual knowledge.

In the earlier days this training was given in suitable surroundings far away from the life of the cities and the teacher was one who had himself passed through the round of this circle of living and, very usually, even one who had arrived at some remarkable realisation of spiritual knowledge. But subsequently education became more intellectual and mundane; it was imparted in cities and universities and aimed less at an inner preparation of character and knowledge and more at instruction and the training of the intelligence. But in the beginning the Aryan man was really prepared in some degree for the four great objects of his life, *dharma, artha, kama, moksa*. Entering into the householder stage to live out his knowledge, he was able to serve there the three first human objects; he satisfied his natural being and its interests and desire to take the joy of life, he paid his debt to the society and its demands and by the way he discharged his life functions he prepared himself for the last greatest purpose of his existence. In the third stage he retired to the forest and worked out in a certain seclusion the truth of his spirit. He lived in a broad freedom from the stricter social bond; but if he so willed, gathering the young around him or receiving the inquirer and seeker, he could leave his knowledge to the new rising generation as an educator or spiritual teacher.

In the last stage of life, he was free to throw off every remaining tie and to wander over the world in an extreme spiritual detachment from all the forms of social life, satisfying only the barest necessities, communing with the universal spirit, making his soul ready for eternity. This circle was not obligatory to all the great majority, never went beyond the first two stages, many passed away in the *vanaprasths* or forest stage. Only the rare few made the last extreme venture and took the life of the wandering recluse. But, this profoundly conceived cycle gave a scheme which kept the full course of the human spirit in its view; it could be taken advantage of by all according to their actual growth and its fullness by those who were sufficiently developed in their present birth to complete the cycle.

On this first firm and noble basis Indian civilization grew to its maturity and became a thing rich, splendid and unique, while it filled the view with the last mountain prospect of a supreme spiritual elevation, it did not neglect the life of the levels. It lived between the busy life of the city and village, the freedom and seclusion of the forest and the last overarching illimitable ether. Moving firmly between life and death it saw beyond both and cut out a hundred high souls, to immortality. It developed the external nature and drew it into the inner self; it enriched life to raise it into the spirit. Thus founded, thus trained, the ancient Indian race grew to astonishing heights of culture and civilization; it lived with a noble, well-based, ample and vigorous order and freedom; it developed a great literature, sciences, arts, crafts, industries; it rose to the highest possible ideals and no mean practice of knowledge and culture, of arduous greatness and heroism, of kindness, philanthropy and human sympathy and oneness; it laid the inspired basis of wonderful spiritual philosophies; it examined the secrets of external nature and discovered and lived the boundless and miraculous truths of the inner being; it fathomed self and understood and possessed the world. As the civilization grew in richness and complexity, it lost indeed the first grand simplicity of its early order.

The intellect towered and widened, but intuition waned or retreated into the hearts of the saints and adepts and mystics. A greater stress came to be laid on scientific system, accuracy and order, not only in all the things of life and mind, but even in the things of the spirit; the free flood of intuitive knowledge was forced to run in his own channels. Society became more artificial and complex, less free and noble; more of a bond on the individual, it was less a field for the growth of his spiritual faculties. The old fine integral harmony gave place to an exaggerated stress on one or other of its elemental factors. *Artha* and *kama,* interest and desire were in some directions developed at the expense of the *dharma*. The lines of the *dharma* were filled and stamped in with so rigid a distinctness as to stand in the way of the freedom of the spirit. Spiritual liberation was pursued in hostility to life and not as its full-orbed result and high crowning. But still some strong basis of the old knowledge remained to inspire, to harmonise, to keep alive the soul of India. Even when deterioration came and a slow collapse, even when the life of the community degenerated into an uneasily petrified ignorance and confusion, the old spiritual aim and tradition remained to sweeten and harmonise and save in its worst days the Indian peoples. For we see that it continually swept back on the race in new waves and high outbursts of life-giving energy or leaped up in intense kindling's of the spiritualised mind or heart, even as it now rises once more in all its strength to give the impulse of a great renascence.

A peculiar figure was the *Rishi,* the man of a higher spiritual experience and knowledge, born in any of the class (caste), but exercising an authority by his spiritual personality over all.... It was a marked feature of the Indian mind that it sought to attach a spiritual meaning and a religious sanction to all, even to the most external social and political circumstances of its life imposing on all classes and functions an ideal, not except incidentally of rights and powers, but odd duties, a rule of their action and an ideal way and temperament, character, spirit in the action, a *Dharma* with a spiritual significance. *It was the work of the Rishi to put his stamp enduringly on the national mind,* to prolong and perpetuate it, to discover and interpret the ideal law and its practical meaning, to cast the life of the people into the well-shaped ideals and significant forms of a civilisation founded on the spiritual and religious sense. And in later ages we find the Brahminic schools of legists attributing their codes, though in themselves only formulations of existing role and custom, to the ancient *Rishis*. Whatever the development of the Indian socio-political body in later days, the original character still exercised its influence, even when all tended to last to become traditionalised and conventionalised instead of moving forward constantly in the steps of a free and living practice.

A greater sovereign in Indian polity than the king (or any political power) was the Dharma, the religious, ethical, social, political, juridic and customary law organically governing the life of the people. This impersonal authority was considered sacred and eternal in its spirit and eternal and the totality of its body, always characteristically the same, the changes organically and spontaneously brought about in its actual form by the evolution of the society being constantly incorporated in it, regional, family and other customs forming a sort of attendant and sub-ordinate body capable of change only from within, and with the *Dharma* no secular authority had any right to autocratic interference.

The religious liberties of the commons were assured and could not be infringed by any secular authority; each religious community, each new or long-standing religion could shape its own way of life and institutions and had its own authorities or governing bodies exercising in their proper field and entire independence. There was no exclusive State religion and the monarch was not the religious head of the people. The social life of the people was similarly free from autocratic interference. Instances of royal legislation in this province are rare and here too, when it occurred, there had to be a consultation of the will of those concerned, as in the rearrangement of the reconstitution of the caste system by the Sena kings in Bengal after its disorganisation during a long period of Buddhist predominance. *Change in the society was brought about not artificially from above but automatically from within and principally by the freedom allowed to families or particular communities to develop or alter automatically their own rule of life, achara.*

The socio-political evolution of Indian civilisation, as far as one can judge from the available records passed through four historical stages, first the simple Aryan community, then a long period of transition in which the national life was proceeding through a considerable variety of experimental formation in political structure and synthesis, thirdly, the definite formation of the monarchial state co-ordinating all the complex elements of the communal life of the people into regional and imperial unities, and last the era of decline in which there was an internal arrest and stagnation and an imposition of new cultures and systems from western Asia and Europe.

The distinguishing character of the first three periods is a remarkable solidity and stability in all the formations and a sound and vital and powerful evolution of the life of the people rendered slow and leisurely by this fundamental conservative stability of the system but all the more sure in its building and living and complete in its structure. And even in its decline this solidity opposes a strong resistance to the process of demolition.

The one principle permanent at the base of construction throughout all the building and extension and rebuilding of the Indian polity was the principle of an organically self-determining communal life, self-determining not only in the mass and by means of the machinery of the vote and a representative body erected on the surface, representative only of the political mind of a part of the nation, which is all that the modern system has been able to manage, but in every pulse of its life and in each separate member of its existence. A free synthetic communal order was its character, and the condition of liberty it aimed at was not so much an individual as a communal freedom.

In the beginning the problem was simple enough as only two kinds of communal units had to be considered, the village and the clan, tribe or small regional people. The free organic life of the first was founded on the system of the self-governing village community and it was done with such sufficiency and solidity that it lasted down almost to our own days resisting all the wear and tear of time and the inroad of other systems and was only recently stream-rollered out of existence by the ruthless and lifeless machinery of the British bureaucratic system. All the people living in its villages mostly on agriculture formed in the total a single religious, social, military, and political body governing itself in its assembly, samiti, under the leadership of the king, as yet without any clear separation of functions or class division of labour.

The agricultural and pastoral life common at first to all the members of the Aryan community, *ksatriya*, remained always the large basis, but it developed an increasingly rich super structure of commerce and industry and numerous arts and crafts and a smaller super structure of specialised military and political and religious and learned occupations and functions. The village community remained throughout the stable unit, the firm grain or indestructible atom of the social body, but there grew up a group life of tens and hundreds of villages, each under its head and needing its administrative organisation, and these, as the clan grew into a large people by conquest or colition with others, became constituents of a kingdom or confederated republican nation, and these again the circles, mandala, of larger kingdoms and finally of one or more great empires. The test of the Indian genius for socio-political construction lay in the successful application of its principle of a communal self-determined freedom and order to suit this growing development and new order of development and new order of circumstances.

The Indian mind evolved, to meet this necessity, the stable socio-religious system of the four orders. Outwardly this might seem to be only a more rigid form of the familiar social system developed naturally in most human peoples at one time or another, a priesthood, a military and political aristocracy, a clan of artisans and free agriculturalists and traders and a proliteriate of serfs or labourers. The resemblance however is only in the externals and the spirit of the system of chaturvarna was different in India.

In the later Vedic and the epic times the fourfold order was at once and inextricably the religious, social, political and economic framework of the society and within that framework each order had its natural portion and in none of the fundamental activities was the share or position of any of them exclusive. This characteristic is vital to an understanding of the ancient system, but has been obscured by false notions formed from a misunderstanding or an exaggeration of later phenomena and of conditions mostly belonging to the decline.

However, a series of religious movements kept up even in the later days. The essential element of the old freedom, brought the highest spiritual knowledge and opportunity to all doors and, as in the beginning we find the Vedic and Vedantic *Rishis* born from all classes, we find too up to the end the Yogins, saints, spiritual thinkers, innovators and restorers, religious poets and singers, the fountain-heads of a living spirituality and knowledge as distinguished from traditional authority and lore, derived from all the strata of the community down to the lowest Shudras and even the despised and oppressed outcastes.

The four orders grew into a fixed social hierarchy, each had attached to it a spiritual life and utility, a certain social dignity, an education, a principle of social and ethical honour and a place and duty and right in the communal body. The system served again an automatic means of securing a fixed division of labour and a settled economic status, the hereditary principle at first prevailing, although here even the theory was more rigid than the practice, but none was denied the right or opportunity of amassing wealth and making some figure in society, administration and politics, by means of influence or status in his own order. For, finally, the social hierarchy was not at the same time a political hierarchy. All the four orders had their part in the common political rights of the citizen and in the assemblies and administrative bodies their place and their share of influence.

The whole Indian system was founded upon a close participation of all the orders in the common life, each predominating in its own field, the *Brahmin* in religion, learning and letters, the *Kshatriya*, in war, king-craft and interstate political action, the *Vaishya* in wealth-getting and productive economical function, but none, not even the *Shudra*, excluded from his share in the civic life and an effective place and voice in politics, administration and justice.

As a consequence, the old Indian polity at no time developed, or at least it did not maintain for long, those exclusive forms of class rule that have so powerfully marked the political history of other countries. A priestly theocracy like that of Tibet, or the rule of a land and military aristocracy that prevailed for centuries in France and England and other European countries or a mercantile oligarchy, as in Carthage and Venice, were the forms of Government foreign to the Indian spirit. A certain political predominance of the great *Kshatriya* families at a time of general war and strife and mobile expansion, when the clans and tribes were developing into nations and kingdoms and were still striving with each other for hegemony and over lordship, seems to be indicated in the traditions preserved in the *Mahabharata* and recurred in a crude form in the return to the clan nation in medieval Rajputana; but in Ancient India this was a passing phase and the predominance did not exclude the political and civic influence of men of the other orders or interfere with or exercise any oppressive control over the free life of the various communal units.

The democratic republics of the intermediate times were in all probability polities which endeveaoured to preserve in its fullness the old principle of the active participation of the whole body of the people in the assemblies and not democracies of the Greece type; the oligarchial republics were clan Governments or were ruled by more limited senates drawn from the dignified elements of the society and this afterwards developed into councils or assemblies representing all the four orders as in the later royal councils and urban bodies. In any case the system finally evolved was a mixed polity in which none of the orders had an undue predominance. Accordingly, we do not find in India either that struggle between the patrician and plebeian elements of the community, the oligarchic and the democratic idea, ending in the establishment of an absolute monarchial rule, which characterises the troubled history of Greece and Rome or that cycle of successive forms evolving by a strife of classes, the regime of the bourgeois industrialising the society and governing and exploiting it in the name of the commons or masses and finally, the present turn towards a rule of the proletariate of Labour, which we see in later Europe.

The summit of political structure was occupied by three governing bodies, the King in his ministerial Council, the metropolitan assembly and the general assembly of the kingdom. The members of the Council and the ministers were drawn from all orders. The Council included a fixed number of *Brahmana*, *Kshatriya*, *Vaishya* and *Shudra* representatives. It is not clear when these great institutions went out of existence, whether before the Mahomedan invasion or as a result of the foreign conquest. In any case the invasion from Central Asia, bringing in a tradition of personal and autocratic rule unfamiliar with these restraints would immediately destroy such bodies, or their remnants or survivals wherever they still existed, and this happened throughout Northern India.

The Indian political system was still maintained for many centuries in the South, but the public assemblies which went on existing there do not seem to have been of the same constitution as the ancient political bodies, but were rather some of the other communal organisations and assemblies of which these were a co-ordination and supreme instrument of control.

These inferior assemblies included bodies orginally of a political character, once the supreme governing institutions of the clan nation, *kula,* and the republic, *gana.* Under the new dispensation they remained in existence , but lost their supreme powers and could only administer with a subordinate and restricted authority the affairs of their constituent communities. The *kula* or clan family persisted, even after it had lost its political character, as a socio-religious institution, especially among the *kshtriyas,* and preserved the tradition of its social and religious law, *kuladharma,* and in some cases its communal assembly, *kula-sangha.*

A stronger permanent element in the Indian communal system, one that grew up in the framework of the four orders—in the end even replacing it—and acquired an extraordinary vitality, persistence and predominance was the historic and still tenacious though decadent institution of caste, *jati.* Originally this rose from sub-divisions of the four orders that grew up in each order under the stress of various forces. The sub-division of the Brahmin castes was mainly due to religious, socio-religious and ceremonial causes, but there were also regional and local divisions; the *Kshtriyas* remained for the most part one united order, though divided into *kulas.*

On the other hand the *Vaishya* and *Shudra* orders split up into innumerable castes under the necessity of economic functions on the basis of the hereditary principle. Apart from the increasingly rigid application of the hereditary principle, this settled sub-division of function well enough have been secured, as in other countries, by a guild system and in towns we do find a vigorous and efficient guild system in existence. But the guild system afterwards fell into destitute and the more general institution of caste became the one basis of economic function everywhere.

The caste in town and in village was a separate communal unit, at once religious, social, and economic, and decided its religious, social and other questions, carried on its caste affairs and exercised jurisdiction over its members in a perfect freedom from all outside interference: only on fundamental questions of the *Dharma* the Brahmins were referred to for an authoritative interpretation or decision as custodians of the *Shastra*. As with the *kula*, each caste had its caste law and rule of living and conduct, *jati-dharma*, and its caste communal assembly, *jati-sangha*. As the Indian polity in all its institutions was founded on a communal and not on an individual basis, the caste also counted in the political and administrative functioning of the kingdom.

The guilds equally were self-functioning mercantile and industrial communal units, assembled for the discussion and administration of their affairs and had besides their united assemblies which seem at one time to have been the governing bodies. These guild Governments, if they may be so called,—for they were more than municipalities,—disappeared afterwards into the more general urban body which represented an organic unity of both the guilds and the caste assemblies of all the order. The castes as such were not directly represented in the general assemblies of the kingdom, but they had their place in the administration of local affairs.

The village community and the township were the most tangibly stable basis of the whole system; but these, it must be noted, were not solely territorial units or a convenient mechanism for electoral, administrative or other useful social and political purposes, but always true communal unities with an organic life of their own that functioned in its own power and not merely as a subordinate part of the machinery of the State. The village community has been described as a little village republic and the description is hardly an exaggeration for each village was within its own limits autonomous and self-sufficient, governed by its own elected Panchayats and elected or hereditary officers, satisfying its own needs, providing for its own education, police, tribunals, all its economic necessities and functions, managing itself its own life as an independent and self-governing unit.

INDIA—MOTHER OF US ALL

India was the motherland of our race and Sanskrit the mother of Europe's Languages. She was the mother of our philosophy, mother through the Arabs of much of our mathematics, mother through Buddha, of the ideals embodied in Christianity, mother through the Village Communities of self-government and democracy. Mother India is in many ways the mother of all of us.

The Role of the Tribal *Savaras* in the Socio-cultural and Religious Movement in Indian Society:

> The land of the *Savaras* in ancient time extended from *Vindhya Mountain in Central India* to *Mahendra Mountain of the Eastern Range*. In *Mahabharata* period this land area was parts of *Dakhina Koshala* and *Kalinga*. The main *Savara* tribes are the *Saoras (Savaras),* the *Kandhas,* the *Gandas,* the *Dumbalas,* the *Binjhalas,* the *Bhuyans,* the *Kolas,* the *Kishnas,* the *Kuras,* the *Kharias,* the *Mundas* and the *Oraons*. In Aryan literature all these tribes are described as the *Savaras*. In pre-Vedic times these tribes were very much advanced. In *Koshala* region they used to live in small groups, each led by a leader who lived in a fort built up of mud or rocks. The ruins of such forts are found in many places. These tribal leaders provided the infrastructural base for administration by people's representatives. In *Dakshina Koshala* these republican entities continued to play their role under the over-lordship of the ruling kings, the most predominant being the *Somavansi* Kings. This republican base maintained the stability of the society during the periods of political turmoils that occurred from time to time.

They are the sons of the soil and lived in harmony with the Nature around them giving a hollow and reverence to every living and non-living entities. They were attached to their environs with emotional and spiritual bonds. They cleared forest, established villages and developed cultivated lands. Near the villages they dug water tanks and reservoirs which are called '*mundas*' in Western Orissa after the name of the tribe '*Munda*'.

They used to keep their valuables (gold, silver, coins) underground. They believed in the existence of divine beings ruling all natural phenomena. These Gods and Goddesses exist everywhere. The names of some of them among the tribes of Western Orissa are: *Verapenu* (Earth God), *Veyetapenu* (Sun God), *Danjupenu* (Moon God), *Sorupenu* (Mountain God), *Dunguripenu* (Hill God), *Gassapenu* (Forest God), *Joripenu* (River God), *Mundapenu* (Tank or Pond God), *Nadayapenu* (Village God), *Sandepenu* (Boundary God), *Lohapenu* (Battle God). There is a tribal custom of installing in each home, village, town and fort a God or Goddess for protection from all calamities. The sanskritised names of these Gods/Goddesses are: *Grihadevata* (Home God), *Gramadevata* (Village God), *Nagaradevata* (Town God), and *Durgadevata* (Fort God). In case of a nation, there was a *Rashtradevata* who took care of the safety and well being of the nation. This custom was not only confined to the tribes but had become prevalent in all the strata of the Indian society.

The idea of *Rashtradevata* is found in the Buddhist *Jatakas* of the 5th or 6th century B.C. In the *Culla Kalinga Jataka,* the *Rashtradevata of Kalinga* and *Asvaka* fought each other in the shape of two bulls, black and white, during the war between the two Kings. The tribal Goddess of the *Savaras* installed in every *Savara* village in the form of a wooden post was the *Rashtradevata* of the *Mahakantara* (present *Kalahandi* and *Bastar* Districts) in the time of Samudra Gupta (326 to 375 A.D.). The Goddess possessed the sanskritised name *Thambheswari* (the Goddess of the Wooden Post).

The *Savaras* of *Kalinga* in ancient time used to instal some stone or wooden post in every hut, every village and every mountain and district. They called their Gods in the generic name of '*Kitung*'. The main '*Kitung*' was installed on the *Mahendra* mountain which was their *Rashtradevata*. Traditionally this place is associated with the *Pandavas* who worshipped this God. There are certain ancient temples on the mountain which are still called *Kunti-deulaa (deula* = temple), *Yudhisthiradeula* and *Bhimadeula, Samudragupta's (326-375 A.D.)* expedition had passed through *Dakshina Koshala,*

Mahakantara, Kurala and *Mahendra*. He selected the top of the *Mahendra* mountain when he liberated the defeated Kings. *Kitung* of the *Savara* Language became Swayambhu in Sanskrit subsequently.

The *Savara* God *Kituing* was subsequently worshipped as *Rashtradevata* by the Matharas (4th century A.D.). *Shailodbhabas* and *Gangas* (11th to 13th century), etc. in different names of the Hindu Pantheon. The *Bhaumakara* Kings (8th to 10th century) of Tosali (present coastal districts of Balasore, Cuttack Puri and part of Ganjarn) embraced Buddhism. So, they introduced the *Mahayana* cult in worshipping the *Rashtradevata 'Swayambhu'* or *'Kitung'* in the name of *Jagannath*. The Jains regard *Jagannath* not as Lord of the Universe but Universe personified. They worship Him also as *Jinanath*. The famous *Savara* Shrine, *Savari-Narayana,* is located on the left bank of the river *Mahanadi* below its junction with the river *Jonk*. According to tradition it was the place where during *Ramayana Period Savari* offered fruits to Rama and got a boon that her name should precede His. So the place is venerated as *Savari-Narayana, Sutra-muni* (Sage *of Shudra* caste) *Sarata Das,* the great 14th century author of Oriya *Mahabharata* traced *Jagannath's* Origin to *Savari-Narayan*. According to him, *Jagannath* was brought to Puri from *Savari-Narayana*.

The Wooden Lord *Jagannatha,* the Lord of the Universe, adorns *Neelachaladham,* the seat on Blue Mountain, at *Shankha-Khetra,* the conch-shaped city, Puri, on the shore *of Mahodadhi,* the Great Sea, the Bay of Bengal. This Seat of the Lord, situated between North and South India across a natural highway along the eastern coast of India, occupies a unique position in the socio-cultural and religious movements of India and displays a grand synthesis, the hall-mark of Indian civilization. It is the holy shrine for the people of every denomination of the indigenous faiths—Tribal, Jainism, Buddhism, Tantricism, Savism, Vaishnavism. Lord Jagannatha bears even today the indelible impress of each of these faiths. What is significant in the Wooden Lord *Jagannatha* is that He is worshipped along with His elder brother Balabhadra and younger sister Subhadra in the Sanctum Sanctorum and that while Lord Jagannath is black, Lord Balabhadra is white and Goddess Subhadra is Yellow. What is most significant in this purely indigenous Indian cultural synthesis is that the tribal *Savaras* have played a crucial and vital role because the God is originally theirs and adopted later successively by others.

Emerging Indian Society

The emerging Indian Society occupies a unique position in the evolutionary process of mankind.

The Evolutionary Destiny of Man

Man was the summit of organic evolution in the cosmic process of evolution. "And with man", says Sir Julian Huxley, the eminent evolutionist, "a new method of evolutionary transformation has come into being, as different from the purely biological method of the natural selection of self-reproducing variants as that was from the methods of inorganic cosmogony". "The human type became a microcosm which through its capacities for awareness, was able to incorporate increasing amounts of the macrocosm into itself, to organise them in new and richer ways, and then with their aid to exert new and more powerful influences on the macrocosm. And the present situation represents a further highly remarkable point in the development of our planet—a critical point at which the evolutionary process, as now embodied in man, has for the first time become aware of itself, is studying the laws of its own unfolding, and has a dawning realisation of the possibilities of its future guidance or control. In other words, evolution is on the verge of becoming internalised, conscious and self-directing".

But it should not be forgotten that, being a product of organic evolution, not only 'the physical memory' transmitted hereditarily from protozoa to man persists in him, but also the memory of the instincts accumulated in the brain which at given times in evolution responded to conditions of existence determined by the evolution. Now these instincts of the bygone ages are not only useless to man but offer great hindrance towards its progress. In the words of Le Comte, "It is against this heredity, against this immense accumulation of memories by now deprived of any meaning, and dating back to epochs forever vanished that man must fight, to prepare the advent of the spiritual being he is destined to become". Thus, man represents, on the one hand, the culmination of organic evolution, and, on the other, the starting point of spiritual evolution.

The purpose of human life is to conquer its digressive animality and direct its life to its evolutionary goal-spiritual existence. *Ishavashyopanishad* proclaimed the path for mankind, '*avidyaya mrityutartwa vidyayamritamashmtte:* conquering this mortal world through science attain immortality through Yoga. Patanjali, in his Yoga aphorism termed the surrounding universe as *drishya,* the Seen and the immortal self of man as *drashta,* the Seer. He defined the Universe, the Seen, as *Prakashakriyasthitishilam bhutendriyatmakam bhogapavargartham drishyam:* 'the Seen is of the nature of illumination, motion and inertia, composed of the elements and organs (non-living and living matter), and meant for the satisfaction of the needs as well as the attainment of supreme freedom.' Science is the knowledge of the cyoernetics of the universe and Yoga is the knowledge of the cybernetics of man. Ancient India knew the importance of both Science and Yoga as well as two goals of human life: *preya* and *shreya. Preya,* life's pleasure, can be attained through Science by harnessing Nature to the service of comfort and luxury. *Shreya,* the Greater Goal is to become the Immortal Free Self and attain the eternal Existence-Knowledge-Bliss. This can be attained through Yoga.

The Evolutionary Goal of Man and the Essence of Indian Social Heritage

This evolutionary goal dawning upon mankind now was the central essence of the Indian social heritage. In the words of Mahayogi Sri Aurobindo, "The master idea that has governed the life, culture, social ideals of the Indian people has been the seeking of man for his true spiritual self and the use of life as a frame and means for that discovery and for man's ascent from the ignorant and natural into the spiritual existence. This dominant idea India has never quite forgotten even under the stress and material exigencies and the externalities of political and economic construction". He has emphasised, "Spirituality is indeed the master key of the Indian mind, the sense of infinity is native to it". "Not peace but fulfilment is what the heart of the world is seeking".

Change under the Impact of Time-Spirit and Continuity of Eternal Values

Needs and responsibilities, ideas and opportunities, heritage and aspiration, time and environment shape paradigm of change and continuity. In the Age of Information Revolution (Cybernetics), Science and Technology, no society can remain unaffected and march against the Time Spirit. But a society endowed with the heritage of the most ancient and continuing culture and civilization can turn the direction of the movement of the Time Spirit towards the evolutionary goal of fulfilment of its own aspiration. This is what is happening today slowly but surely. People throughout India are:

- adapting to modern circumstances keeping to traditional social pattern,
- altering little the fundamental motifs of cognition and motivation,
- sticking to their respective *jati* or caste which continues to be the attribute of identity, the principal unit of endogamy, vehicle of social interaction and mobility, political motivation,
- becoming liberal so far as caste tradition is concerned and are becoming diversified in occupation, education, income, and residence,
- working, when opportunities are available, outside their home localities and in activities for which *jati* considerations are irrelevant.

Other trends of change perceptible are:

- social order in villages continues to be perceived as being made up of ranked, interdependent *jatis,* but the criteria of ranking and the meaning of interdependence seem to be in the process of revision,

- the cultural and social distances among *jatis* are shrinking; the *sanskritic* tradition as well as modern tradition of the elite and educated are becoming accessible to the lowest *jatis;* they are becoming aware of their high cultural tradition and social, political and economical potentialities of reaching to any position in field, which have been attained by individuals from their ranks,
- the elected village *panchayats* are becoming established as local agencies for economic development and social enhancement.
- tensions arising out of change and counter-change in the status of rank, a sign of social fossilisation and inertia for a past millennium, is a passing phase, and a step towards the attainment of a greater harmony and stability, Gandhiji's *Gram Swaraj* or Village Republic.

Continuity and Sustainability of the Eternal Values in an age of devastating change:

- the eternal value system which have sustained Indian society throughout the ages since the beginning of human civilization remains intact and provide and will continue to provide sustenance and stability to the society,
- a person of values, especially a spiritually evolved soul, belonging to any caste, lowest of the low, commands greater respect from the society than others, however great they may be,
- free play of inner freedom of Spirit. "The ambition of a particular religious belief and form to universalise and impose itself is contrary to the variety of human nature and to at least on essential character of the Spirit. For the nature of the Spirit is a spacious inner freedom and a large unity into which each man must be allowed to grow according to his own nature".

Mission and Aspiration of Indian Society

The Great Seer Sri Aurobindo has proclaimed: "India is the *Bharata Shakti*, the living energy of a great spiritual conception and fidelity to it is the very principle of her existence. For by its virtue alone she has been one of the immortal nation, this alone has been the secret of her amazing persistence and perpetual force of survival and revival". "Spiritual and temporal have Indeed to be perfectly harmonised, for the spirit works through mind and body. But the purely intellectual or heavily material culture of the kind that Europe (West) now favours bears in its heart the seed of death."

"The lifeless attempt of the last generation to imitate and reproduce with a servile fidelity the Ideals and forms of the West has been no true indication of the political mind and genius of the Indian people. But again amid all the mist of confusion there is still the possibility of a new twilight, not of an evening but a morning *yuga-sandhya*. India of the ages is not dead nor has she spoken her last creative word; she lives and has still something to do for herself and the human people. And that, which must seek now to awake is not an anglicised orient people, docile pupil of the West and doomed to repeat the occident's success and failure, but still the ancient immemorable *Shakti* recovering her deepest self, lifting her head higher towards the supreme source of light and strength and turning to discover the complete meaning and a vaster form of her Dharma."

In trying circumstances throughout the ages in the past, Indian society preferred *shreya* to *preya* and neglected science, and lost political freedom, but not, never the freedom of its soul. Bhatruhari of the Classical Age in his *Nitishatakam* warned human society, 'Those persons who have no wisdom, no austerity, no contribution, no knowledge, no refined behaviour, no qualities, no *dharma,* they are, in this mortal world, a big burden to the earth.' Today Indian society is awakening to the importance of both science and yoga. For Today's world, Gandhiji's message was peace and non-violence. The Great Gandhian Vinoba Bhave termed the present time as *the Age of Science and Yoga* which together can usher harmony within human society and between human society and environment and fulfil human aspiration.

The supreme aspiration of Indian society is to attain fulfillment through the realisation of the message of the Great Seer Sri Aurobindo, "The problems which have troubled mankind can only be solved by conquering the kingdom within, not by harnessing the forces of Nature to the service of comfort and luxury, but by mastering the forces of the intellect and the spirit, by vindicating the freedom of man from within as well as without and conquering from within external Nature."

Bibliography

Aggarwal, J.C. (1999): *Theory and Principles of Education*, Vikas Publishing House Pvt. Ltd., New Delhi.

Altaker, A.S. (1964): *Education in Ancient India*, Orient Longman Pvt. Ltd., Bombay.

Banton, M. Roles (1965): *An Introduction to the Study of Social Relations*, (Tavistock).

Basu, A.N. (1965): *Education in Modern India*, Asia Publishing House, New Delhi.

Capra, Fritzof (1982): *The Turning Point, Science Society and the Rising Culture,* Flamingo, Fontaena Paperback, 1989.

CBSE (1996): *Learning the Treasure With*, Report to UNESCO of the International Commission on Education for the 21st Century, CBSE, New Delhi.

Chalam, K.S. (1993): *Educational Policy for Human Resources Development*, Rawat Publications, Jaipur.

Chaman Lal (ed.) (1968): *India Mother of Us All,* Bhikshu Chaman Lal Modern School, New Delhi.

Chandlel, Kenneth (1987): "Modern Science and Vedic Science: An Introduction," *Modern Science and Vedic Science*, Vol. I. No. 4. Maharishi International University, Fairfield, Iowa.

Davis, K. (1948): *Human Society,* Macmillan, New York.

Dhiman, O.P. (1987): *Foundation of Education*, Atma Ram & Sons, Delhi.

Faure E. et al. (1972): *Learning to Be: The World of Education*, Today and Tomorrow.

Garan, Stanely Marion (1963): "The Races of Mankind," *The Book of Popular Science*, Vol. 8.

Gautier, Francois (1996): *Rewritting Indian History*, Vikash Publishing House Pvt. Ltd., New Delhi.

Guru, G. and Singh, D.P. (ed.) (1996): "Environment and Development", *A Textbook of Environmental Education and Rural Development*, NCERT, New Delhi.

Jafer, S.M. (1960): *Education in Muslim India*, Asia Publishing House, Bombay.

Johnson, H.M. (1961): *Sociology: A Systematic Introduction*, Routledge and Kegan Paul.

Kabir, Humayun (1963): *Education in New India*, Orient Longman.

Kalidasa (Classical Sanskrit Poet): *Kumarsambhava* (The First Verse).

Macionis, John J. (4th Edn. 1998): *Society, the Basics,* Prentice Hall, New Jersey, USA.

Maharishi, Mahesh Yogi (1996): *India to be the Supreme Power in the World,* Maharishi Mahesh Yogi Vedic Vishwavidyalaya, Maharana Pratap Nagar, Bhopal (MP).

Mandel Baum, David G. (1970): *Society in India*, Popular Prakashan, Mumbai, 2000.

Mazumdar, N.N. (1961): *Education in Ancient India*, Publication Division, New Delhi.

MHRD (1986): *National Policy on Education*, Govt. of India, New Delhi.

Mitchell, G.D. (ed) (1968): *A Dictionary of Sociology*, Routledge and Kegan Paul.

Mukherjee, R.K. (1963): *Ancient Indian Education*, Acharya Book Depot, Baroda.

Munshi, K.M. (1961): *Foundation of Indian Culture*, Bhartiya Vidya Bhawan, Chowpatty, Mumbai, 1965.

Narullah, S. and Naik, J.N.: *A History of Education in India.*

NCERT (1986): *School Education in India: Present Status and Future Needs*, New Delhi.

New Education Policy, 1986.

Rasskh, S. and Vaideanu, G. (1987): *The Content of Education*, Sterling Publishing, New Delhi.

Report of Education Commission, 1964-66.

Report of Secondary Education Commission, 1953.

Report of Universities Education Commission, 1999.

Saiyaaidain, K.G. (1962): *Compulsory Education in India*, Asia Publishing House, Bombay.

Shane, H.G. (1977): *Curriculum Change Towards the Twenty-First Century*, National Education Association, Washington D.C.

Singh, K. (2000): *Education for Global Society*, The Academic Journal of the Doon School, Vol. I, Issue 5, Spring 200, Dehradoon.

Sorokin, P.A. (1948): *Reconstruction of Humanity*, Kraus Reproduced (Fascimile).

Sri Aurobindo (1909-10): *The Ideal of Karmyogi*, Sri Aurobindo Ashram Trust, Sri Aurobindo Ashram, Pondicherry.

Sri Aurobindo (1916-20): *Human Cycle, War and Self Determination*, Sri Aurobindo Ashram, Pondicherry, 1962.

Sri Aurobindo (1920): *Ideals and Progress*, Sri Aurobindo Ashram Trust, Sri Aurobindo Ashram, Pondicherry.

Sri Aurobindo Society (1996): *A New Approach to Education*, Sri Aurobindo Institute of Research in Social Sciences, Sri Aurobindo Society, Pondicherry.

Sri Swami Sivananda (1947): *All About Hinduism*, The Divine Life Society, Shivananda Nagar, Rishikesh, Himalaya, 1961.

The Central Gazetteer, Govt. of India (1965): *The Gazetteer of India, Indian Union*, Vol. I, *Country and People*, Publication Division, Ministry of Information and Broadcasting, Govt. of India, New Delhi.

Toffler, A. (1970): *Future Shock*, The Bodly Head, London.

Toffler, A. (1981): *The Third Wave*, Buntam Books, Torento.

Toffler, A. (ed) (1978): *Learning for Tomorrow: The Role of the Future in Education*, Random House, New York.

UNESCO (1982): *World Problem in the Classroom*, UNESCO, Paris.